Winwick Manor House.

Shire County Guide 22

NORTHAMPTONSHIRE

Jack Gould

Shire Publications Ltd

CONTENTS

Printed in Great Britain by C. I. Thomas & Sons (Haverfordwest) Ltd, Press Buildings, Merlins Bridge, Haverfordwest, Dyfed.

British Library Cataloguing in Publication Data available.

ACKNOWLEDGEMENTS
The author gratefully acknowledges the help given in the writing of this book by the following: Christine Cole, Marian Pipe, Geoffrey Starmer and Lou Warwick; Northamptonshire Leisure and Libraries Department; Northamptonshire Wildlife Trust; District Council offices at Corby, Daventry, East Northants, Kettering, South Northants and Wellingborough; information offices at Northampton and Oundle; the *Northampton Chronicle and Echo* and its writer on local history, Alan Burman.

Photographs are acknowledged as follows: *Chronicle and Echo,* pages 6, 17, 19 (left), 24, 35, 37, 39 (left), 45, 46, 51, 53, 54, 55 and 57 (left); Compton Estates, page 26; Mary Gould, page 48; Des Richardson, pages 57 (right) and 66; Fred Sutton, pages 10 and 38; Lou Warwick, pages 7 and 63; all the rest are by Cadbury Lamb. The map on page 65 is by D. R. Darton.

Cover: *Great Weldon church.*

Harlestone village.

1
The lie of the land

A passenger in a car going north on the M1 motorway crosses nearly 30 miles (50 km) of Northamptonshire. In doing so she or he might think it somewhat unexciting, since from Salcey Forest on the Buckinghamshire border to the viaduct over the river Avon at the boundary of Leicestershire there are no dramatic features along the way. To a keen eye there are, however, a number of pointers to the unobtrusive pleasures of the county.

Salcey Forest, through the western edge of which the motorway cuts a swathe, is the smallest of three ancient royal forests and along with Whittlewood and Rockingham covered much of Northamptonshire in medieval times. Sizeable areas of these forests still exist and since large parts of them are in the charge of the Forestry Commission there is free access in many places (chapter 2).

Next, on the western side, is the trim estate of Courteenhall, the seat of Major Sir Here-ward Wake, MC, Baronet, who can reckon 28 generations of ancestors from Geoffrey Wac, who held lands in Normandy. The family has been in Northamptonshire since the thirteenth century and their presence and that of others like them has led to its being called the 'county of spires and squires'.

After Junction 15 comes Collingtree on the eastern side, where the motorway defines the limit of expanded Northampton (chapter 10). Past the Rothersthorpe service station, the tall silos of the flour mills at Bugbrooke rise above the flood plain of the river Nene, which is a dominant feature in so much of Northampton-shire.

John Norden said of the county in his *Delineation of Northamptonshire* early in the seventeenth century: 'It lieth in a plain forme, not craggie by reason of extraordinarie high hills, fells, or mountaines, though some ascendings and descendings theare are . . .' Having passed Junction 16, where the A45 crosses the motorway, an 'ascending' can be seen in the rounded contours of Borough Hill, bristling with masts and hiding Daventry from view (chapter 3).

The Grand Union Canal is a quiet but considerable presence and the seven locks at Whilton and Buckby Wharf are close on the western side, where along with their associated buildings and bridges they make a pleasant piece of canalscape.

At the Blue Boar service station it can be

3

seen that three other trunk routes to the north-west are close by. The Roman engineers came this way with the Watling Street, as did the builders of the Grand Junction Canal, and Robert Stephenson followed the same line with the London and Birmingham Railway. Like the M1 engineers, they chose this route to cross the Northamptonshire uplands at their narrowest point. The hills, which run along the west flank of the county, have been a barrier through the ages and the Watford Gap is the easiest way through. Their rounded undulations — Arbury Hill near Badby at 734 feet (224 metres) is the highest — have a greater importance than their appearance suggests. They are part of the limestone ridge running from south-west to north-east across England from the Mendips via the Cotswolds through Northamptonshire to the Lincolnshire and Yorkshire Wolds. The scarp on the western side provides some of the most distant vistas in the county, such as Honey Hill near Cold Ashby, from where you can look a long way into Warwickshire. The limestone has provided good building material through the ages and the infusion of iron in some places has tinged it with a warmer blush than the pale grey Cotswold variety.

The Reverend John Morton, in his *Natural History of Northamptonshire* (1712), wrote of one of the county's great glories, the churches in the Nene valley from Easton Maudit to Titchmarsh, 'each with a lofty spire' by which

it appeared 'how plentifully we are stor'd with Quarrystone. Just uncovering the earth in some places they take up stone that's every way fit for building.' The truth of this is still apparent, although most of the quarries have closed. Even so, Weldon, which provided stone for the building of Castle Ashby House between 1574 and 1640 and innumerable other edifices down the years, is still in business. Another famous quarry was at Barnack, where the 'hills and holes' testify to the extraction of the 'freestone' that helped to build many medieval cathedrals. This was in the Soke or Liberty of Peterborough, attached to Northamptonshire until 1880 but now part of Cambridgeshire, although by a typically English quirk northern parts of the county fall within the parliamentary constituency of Peterborough.

Ironstone has also been important. Domesday Book mentions 'iron-workings' at Corby and Gretton before the Norman conquest, but it was from the nineteenth century onwards that much 'getting' of ironstone took place and in 1932 began the rapid rise of Corby (chapter 10).

The inconsiderable Northamptonshire heights are one of the greatest watersheds in central England. The rivers Welland and Avon both rise near Naseby and flow in opposite directions to end in the Wash and the Bristol Channel respectively. The Great Ouse and its tributary the Tove begin in the Brackley

The ironworks at Corby in 1979.

region and travel eastward; the Leam near Hellidon flows west to join the Avon and the Cherwell from Charwelton goes south to meet the Thames. They all provide the county boundary in their several places.

But the river which dominates and whose valley is the most prominent feature of the county is the Nene ('Nenn' at Northampton and 'Neen' lower down). The shape of the county has been likened to a leaf and the river to its midrib. The total length of the Nene is 115 miles (184 km) and it flows throughout most of the county from south-west to north-east. Only the south-west corner, in the catchment area of the Ouse and Cherwell, is remote from the Nene or one of its tributaries. Rising near Staverton, it falls rapidly at first — 300 feet (90 metres) in 17 miles (27 km) — but after joining another arm at Northampton it winds down a wide flood plain on its way to the Wash. Along the river's course and that of its tributary the Ise are nearly all the main centres of population. Corby, which was specially developed, is the only large town removed from its influence. At Northampton the river is joined by the Gayton arm of the Grand Union Canal, thus giving access from the main central canal system (chapter 7). From 1761 onwards the river was made navigable up to the county town and although it fell into disuse and decrepitude after the coming of the railways the Nene Catchment Board made it once more viable in the 1930s, so that it can be enjoyed by the owners of pleasure craft.

Some of the feeders of the Nene were used to create reservoirs, as at Ravensthorpe, Hollowell and Sywell, which now seem almost natural features. The creation of much larger storage lakes since the Second World War, such as Pitsford (chapter 2) and outside the county at Grafham and Empingham (Rutland Water), as part of the Anglia Water Board's huge supply system has made Sywell redundant and with its surroundings it is being made into a country park (chapter 2).

In the middle ages there were great royal hunting forests in Northamptonshire: Whittlewood and Salcey in the south, on the boulder clay of the waterlogged plateau between the Nene and Ouse valleys, and Rockingham in the north between the Nene and the Welland. These attracted visits by medieval monarchs. Although they are now much shrunken there are still considerable tracts of woodland where the Forestry Commission has provided facilities for visitors (chapter 2).

Another and distinctive region in the county is the wold country between Brackley and Towcester (pronounced 'Toaster'), on the west side of the Watling Street. The rolling terrain here is mostly between 400 and 500 feet (130-70 metres) and is thinly populated with stone-built villages, many of which, such as Blakesley, Culworth and Lois Weedon (this is the name as the inhabitants prefer it, rather than Weedon Lois), are very picturesque.

The area is crossed by the ancient prehistoric trackway known to modern historians as the Jurassic Way, believed to have led from the Mendips along the limestone spine as far north as the Yorkshire Wolds. The rise in importance of Banbury in medieval times caused parts of the way to be used as a droving road and along the Banbury Lane came countless beasts on their way to Northampton and the Midland pastures.

About 2 miles (3 km) of the track near Moreton Pinkney and Adstone have never been metalled and survive as a remnant of green lane and a reminder of its earlier condition. The open uncrowded countryside around here makes one think of the locality as the 'empty quarter' of the county and its atmosphere and the enjoyable walking in the area make it for many a favourite part of Northamptonshire. It has another recommendation for 'real ale' enthusiasts: it is in the territory of the Hook Norton Brewery, not far away in Oxfordshire.

Size and location

The county is smaller than average with 585,000 acres (250,000 ha). It is just under 60 miles (96 km) from north to south and nowhere more than 40 miles (64 km) from east to west. Before the Local Government Act of 1974 it bordered more counties than any other — nine in all. This position gives reason to dispute the claim of Meriden in West Midlands to be the very centre of England and a case can be made out for the Daventry district, which is why early radio transmissions came from Borough Hill.

There is, however, an East Anglian connection. The north-east corner of the county approaches the Fens; during the Civil War Northampton was a Parliamentary stronghold on the flank of the Eastern Association and today it falls within the region of Anglia Television.

In medieval times the strategic central situation of the town of Northampton gave it great national importance. Thomas Fuller, the antiquarian and divine who was born at Aldwincle and wrote the *Worthies of England*, said of the county town: 'so impartial is the situation in the navel of the kingdom'. Royalty often used the great castle (chapter 3) and parliaments met in the town in the fourteenth century.

After the middle ages Northampton's national importance declined and it was not until Victorian times, when the boot and shoe industry grew enormously, that the town became once more prominent. Although in 1642 a large order of footwear for the army going to Ireland was placed in the town and in

5

1662 Fuller made the celebrated statement that 'the town of Northampton may be said to stand chiefly on other mens' legs', it was only with the coming of the canal in 1815 and the railway in 1845 that large-scale expansion of the trade began. From 7000 in 1801, the population of the town rose to 30,000 in 1851 and by the end of the nineteenth century reached 87,000. It was during those years that Northampton's name became synonymous with the craft of boot and shoe making.

Other and smaller towns in the county likewise but later grew apace for the same reason. Rushden in 1871 had a population of just over 2000 and forty years later had reached 13,000, while Kettering rose from just over 5000 in 1851 to nearly 30,000 in 1911.

Although cheap foreign imports have cut into the mass-produced trade, many firms flourish, especially in the 'up-market' sector. Also Northampton, Wellingborough and Daventry in particular have expanded further because of their position in relation to modernised railways and the national motorway system. After the M1 was opened in 1959 Northampton became a 'hub town' in the modern jargon. Its position about halfway along the London to Birmingham corridor and population overspill from the capital have led to massive expansion. A development corporation set up in Northampton in 1968 brought about growth at a phenomenal speed.

Daventry expanded fast in 1967-8 with help from Birmingham and more slowly since, and Wellingborough grew with the assistance of the Greater London Council from 1967 to 1980.

In 1961 the combined population of the borough of Northampton and the county of Northamptonshire was in round figures 398,000. By 1987 this had increased by about 150,000. Even so, compared with some counties the population is still sparse and the county has retained its rural character. Away from the M1 and the main centres of population large tracts of unspoiled countryside persist, where traffic is light and villages built mainly from multicoloured stone are attractively disposed amongst fertile fields and well kept woodland. The plenitude of good building stone has given rise to churches second to none and mansions set in noble parkland that equal any in England.

In the past Northamptonshire tended to be an unconsidered county, through which travellers passed, unless they were keen on churches or stately homes, on their way to more exciting regions. Now it has been called the 'Rose of the Shires'. This is partly to do with the county insignia of the Tudor rose but also suggests the unobtrusive treasures that await those prepared to stop and stare. It is hoped that this brief guide will point the way for people who wish to do just that.

The Barratt shoe factory.

6

A seventeenth-century view of Northampton.

2
The countryside

Fuller wrote of the fertile soil of Northampton-shire and of the paucity of 'waste ground' — in other words 'no mosses, meres, fells, heaths' — and this means that one cannot roam in the way possible in Cornwall or Yorkshire. There are, though, a number of pleasant places where the tolerance of private landowners or the efforts of various councils, the Forestry Commission or the Northamptonshire Wildlife Trust make it possible for people to relax in the countryside.

Badby Wood, near Daventry (OS 152; SP 565585). About ½ mile (800 metres) east from the A361 along the road to Everdon.

This privately owned woodland consists of 181 acres (72 ha) of deciduous woodland, to most of which the Fawsley Estate allows public access. A stone gateway, formerly part of a lodge, commands the entrance to the wood. If possible park beside the road and approach by the field path. Another way is to park in the village and enter the wood via the county footpath, the Knightley Way (see below). Badby Wood is a very popular spot so it is best to visit at quiet periods. There is a great variety of trees and many paths between them. In spring the ground is carpeted with bluebells.

Barnwell Country Park, near Oundle (OS 141; SP 033873). Telephone: Oundle (0832) 73435. Off the old A605 just south of Oundle, on the way to Thrapston.

This county council country park of 37 acres (15 ha) is based on one of several flooded gravel pits along the Nene valley adapted for leisure use. The deposits were created at the end of the last ice age, when following the rapid thaw the Nene became a mighty torrent a mile (1.5 km) wide and carried vast quantities of sand and gravel. These resources have been heavily worked in the Oundle and Thrapston area and the Barnwell pit was dug from 1957 to 1968. The park was established in 1970/1. A great variety of habitat is present: woodland with many willows, meadows, marshy ground and open water. 32 species of birds nest regularly there and many visit. Day-permit fishing includes facilities for disabled anglers and there are picnic meadows and waterside walks with a warden and information service.

Brigstock Country Park, near Corby (OS 141; SP 955850). Telephone: Brigstock (053 673) 625. A county council park, off the A6116, beside the Brigstock bypass and the ancient Harley Way to Oundle.

Brigstock was an important forest village in Rockingham Forest (chapter 10). The park has the same area as Barnwell and has picnic meadows and walks through thorn scrub around a former sandpit. There is a warden and information service.

Bucknell Wood, near Silverstone (OS 152; SP 650450). Forestry Commission. ½ mile (800 metres) along the by-road from the A43 at Silverstone to Abthorpe.

An outlier of Whittlewood (Whittlebury Forest), the wood consists of mainly deciduous woodland with numerous 'ridings' where walking is easy and pleasant except in wet weather. There is a wide variety of wild flowers (see Salcey Forest). A car park adjoins the road and a picnic place is to be found further into the wood.

Daventry Country Park, Welton Road, Daventry (OS 152; SP 575637). Telephone: Daventry (0327) 77193.

Daventry District Council has created this 134 acre (54 ha) park around a Grand Union Canal feeder reservoir which has existed since about 1800 and so appears to be part of the landscape. There are picnic sites, waterside walks, a nature trail and an adventure playground. Work is proceeding on an old canal house to create an information centre and meeting place.

Denford Churchyard, near Thrapston (OS 141; TL 992767). On the A605 between Raunds and Thrapston.

The Northamptonshire Wildlife Trust has more than twenty nature reserves (see under Lings Wood). Denford is closer to the river Nene than most villages, which are usually separated from it by the wide flood plain. The churchyard is on a knoll just above the river, so the herbage is of particular interest and very attractive to butterflies and birds.

East Carlton Countryside Park, near Corby (OS 141; SP 832896). Telephone: Rockingham (0536) 770977. On the A427 road from Corby to Market Harborough.

Created by the district council, East Carlton is a very well appointed park centred on the former home of the Palmer family, who in 1873 built a hall in the style of a French *château*. The 100 acres (40 ha) of parkland overlook the valley of the river Welland. Within it are play and picnic areas, a water garden, an alpine garden and three nature trails of varying lengths. On these trails can be

seen an outcrop of the ironstone seam that led to the growth of the local iron and steel industry. The former coach-house is now an industrial heritage centre illustrating features of that industry (chapter 6).

Farthinghoe Nature Reserve, near Middleton Cheney (OS 151; SP 518404). The entrance to the reserve is beside the bridge carrying the minor road from Thenford to Purston over the old railway cutting.

This Northamptonshire Wildlife Trust reserve is in a cutting on what was formerly the Banbury to Buckingham railway line. The county council bought the section in 1965 to use as an infill site but it has now been adapted for more salubrious use. The 8 acre (3 ha) reserve contains low thorn scrub ideal for nesting warblers, a damp meadow favouring many butterfly species, grassland where drifts of moon daisies and other meadow flora are seen in spring and summer, a wet ditch supporting watercress beds and reed-mace and a wide variety of tree and shrub species. At some points there are wide views over the Purston Brook and the Cherwell valley into which it flows.

Fawsley Park, near Daventry (OS 152; SP 565568). Approached from the A361 Banbury to Daventry road along a minor road a mile (1.5 km) north of Charwelton.

Fawsley is the former seat of the Knightley family. In the park the great hall and the solitary church of St Mary, containing a number of Knightley tombs, face a pleasant prospect. The Knightleys were here for more than four hundred years and were once great enclosers, so that Fawsley, Snorscomb and other villages were depopulated. The site of Fawsley village lies under the curving double lake created by 'Capability' Brown. Between the lakes and across the parkland goes the county footpath, the Knightley Way (see below). Charles I hunted in the park before the battle of Naseby. Nowadays it is a more popular resort, so that as parking is limited it is best not to go there at bank holidays and other busy times.

Finedon Country Park (OS 141; SP 913723).

Opened in October 1987, the 35 acre (14 ha) site stretches from Station Road in Finedon towards Burton Latimer and, like the park at Irchester, is based on old ironstone workings, including considerable lengths of mineral railway track. Wellingborough Borough Council bought the land and it is managed by Finedon Parish Council.

The Grafton Way (OS 152; SP 670499).

This was the second county footpath to be opened — in 1975 — and continues from the

The bucket from an iron digger in East Carlton Countryside Park.

Knightley Way for 11½ miles (18.5 km) mostly by field paths, from near the church at Greens Norton. At its southern end it links with the North Bucks Way at the county boundary near Cosgrove. Its name derives from the Dukes of Grafton, whose seat was at Wakefield Lawn near Potterspury, one of the villages on the route. They were great landowners locally from the eighteenth century until shortly after the First World War (chapters 5 and 10). Among other interesting features along the way is the Queen's Oak. An illustrated map of the track is available from the Leisure and Libraries Department of the county council.

Harlestone Heath (OS 152; SP 712636). On the A428 between New Duston and Harlestone there is a long lay-by on the western side of the road and almost opposite the track that leads past a lodge into the heath.

Long before country parks were thought of local folk enjoyed themselves in that part of Earl Spencer's estate more commonly known to them as Harlestone Firs. Despite Fuller's statement that there were no heaths in the county a few did exist, such as here and at Lings Wood (see below). As the soils on this part of the Althorp estate are predominantly sandy many Scots pines were planted along with a good mixture of broad-leaved species over an area of about 1 mile (1.5 km) square, between the A428 road and the Northampton to Rugby railway line. There are many footpaths and bridleways and the sandy soil makes

walking easier than over the clay terrain more typical of the county.

Hunsbury Hill Country Park, Northampton (OS 152; SP 738584). 1¼ miles (2.5 km) south-west of the town centre, approached from Danes Camp Way dual carriageway, part of the ring road system, following the sign to Camp Hill.

The country park is centred on the iron age hillfort (see chapter 3) which is locally called Danes Camp. Camp Hill is the name of a housing estate built in 1987. One flank of the hill has been attractively landscaped and there is much interest here historically and in what is happening today (chapter 7). There is a picnic area commanding spectacular views over the townscape of Northampton. Climbing the side of the hill and cleverly integrated into the park is the original track of the Banbury Lane (chapter 1), surviving as a green lane.

Irchester Country Park, Irchester (OS 152; SP 910660). Telephone: Wellingborough (0933) 76866. Adjoining the B570, which leaves the A509 2 miles (3.5 km) south of Wellingborough.

This large park of 200 acres (81 ha) is in a former ironstone quarry where trees, mainly larch and Scots pine, were planted on the 'hills and dales' resulting from the old working method, so that with later additions of alder and poplar there is a good range of woodland. The park was opened in 1971 and includes a

The church at Fawsley is passed by the Knightley Way.

picnic area, nature trail, a 2 mile (3 km) 'perimeter trail', a shorter trail suitable for wheelchairs and a children's playground. There is a warden and information service and pamphlets covering almost every aspect of the park's ecology are on sale. The park is of great importance in connection with the industrial archaeology of ironstone quarrying (chapter 7).

Kinewell Lake Nature Reserve, Ringstead, near Thrapston (OS 141; SP 980752). Immediately west of Ringstead off the A605 and beside a minor road that crosses the river Nene en route to Great Addington.

Like others along the course of the Nene, the lake originated from gravel extraction. It covers 50 acres (20 ha), with islands, while 80 acres (32 ha) of adjacent land have been incorporated in the scheme. It was named after a spring that is now submerged. Remarkably, the nature reserve is the product of village endeavour led by the Ringstead Parish Council. A trust was set up, more than fifteen hundred trees and shrubs were planted, picnic tables and seats installed and a car park made. A channel cut through to the river keeps the lake full and stocked with fish and many birds are attracted, so that the county record for the largest sighting of avocets was achieved here. A silhouette of the great crested grebe was chosen as a symbol of this story of successful village enterprise.

Knightley Way (OS 152; SP 561587).

The first 'county path' was opened in 1972 and follows public rights of way from Badby to Greens Norton over a distance of 12 miles (19 km). Badby is an attractive village close by the A361 2 miles (3 km) south of Daventry and has a youth hostel in a seventeenth-century cottage on Church Green. The path starts from Church Hill and crosses Fawsley Park on its way through Preston Capes, Mantles Heath, where there is a good prospect across the upper Nene valley and on to Farthingstone ('Farraxton' in the vernacular), where the Red Lion makes an agreeable halfway house. It continues through Litchborough, crossing the Banbury Lane at Foxley, and finally to Greens Norton, beckoned on in the last stages by the church spire added in the eighteenth century to make an eyecatcher for the great house at Easton Neston.

Lings Wood Nature Trail, Northampton (OS 152; SP 802636). Telephone: Northampton (0604) 405285. 5 miles (8 km) from the town centre near the A4500 road to Wellingborough, in part of the Eastern Development of the town. Lings Way leads from the main road to the point of access.

Lings House in Lings Wood is the headquarters of the Northamptonshire Wildlife Trust. Visitors are welcome to look at the displays and learn about the work of the voluntary organisation and charity which aims to protect

10

wildlife in the county. Lings Wood covers 56 acres (23 ha). As its name implies, in the sixteenth century it was heather (or ling) and gorse heathland but there is now mixed woodland and lawns around the house. Some of the soil consists of acid Northampton Sands, unusual in this district. Bracken and rhododendrons dominate the ground flora in places and foxgloves grow. All three species of woodpecker and many other resident and visiting birds are seen and heard, and a large number of different butterflies and other insects are present, especially on the open spaces and lawns. Leaflets describing the nature trail can be bought at the shop in Lings House.

Market Harborough Railway Line Linear Park (OS 152; SP 737653).

Created in 1987, this country park starts from the Boughton level crossing where the railway formerly crossed the A50 road 4 miles (6.5 km) north of Northampton town centre. It is possible to walk the 15¼ miles (26 km) from here to the Leicestershire border immediately south of Market Harborough. The county once had a network of branch lines, but of eighty stations only six survive. The line from Market Harborough to Northampton was the last to close and has been acquired by the county council. Further facilities are planned to afford maximum use of the linear park.

Northamptonshire Nene Way (OS 152; SP 561587).

When complete it is hoped that the Nene Way will be 67 miles (108 km) long, starting at Badby youth hostel (on the Knightley Way, above) and ending at Wansford with a continuation to join Peterborough's Nene Way. In 1987 the section from Badby via Newnham, Weedon Bec, Flore, Nether Heyford and Kislingbury to Northampton was opened.

Pitsford Reservoir (OS 152; SP 760687). Telephone: Manager's Office, Anglian Water Authority, Northampton (0604) 781350. 7 miles (11 km) north of Northampton, close to the A508 road to Market Harborough.

The reservoir was one of the first generation of large reservoirs built since the Second World War and is about 3 miles (5 km) long. The area at water level is 740 acres (300 ha) and the perimeter measures 13 miles (21 km). The reservoir holds nearly 4000 million gallons (18 million cubic metres) of water. This artificial lake is used for sailing and fishing for brown and rainbow trout, with classes for beginners taught by expert instructors. The Scaldwell and Walgrave arms of the reservoir comprise one of the county Wildlife Trust's reserves and its 250 acres (100 ha) are very important for wildfowl and passage migrants,

over two hundred species having been recorded, including teal, widgeon, pochard, tufted duck and great crested grebe.

One public car park is near the Holcot causeway, where the road to that village crosses, and the other on a minor road going down from Pitsford village. Tracks and walks exist around parts of the reservoir's perimeter. The water has covered a tract of Pytchley Hunt territory and on the A508 half a mile (800 metres) from its western end is a monument to one of the many aristocratic followers of the chase. Charles Compton, third Baron Chesham, was killed hunting in 1907 and his memorial says that he was 'a good man, a gallant soldier, a true sportsman'.

Salcey Forest (OS 152; SP 800520). Forestry Commission. On the border of Buckinghamshire and Northamptonshire between the M1 and the B526 road from Northampton to Newport Pagnell, from which it is most easily accessible.

Whereas the larger forests of Whittlewood and Rockingham are now fragmented, Salcey remains a compact unit about 2 miles (3 km) long from north to south and 1½ miles (2.5 km) east to west, with 1300 acres (520 ha) of woodland encircling Salcey Lawn. The Lawn is an open space of about 250 acres (100 ha) which once afforded grazing for the one thousand deer which inhabited the forest until the Enclosure Act of 1825 but it is now private farmland.

In 1986 Salcey ended its long-time role as a game preserve when the pheasant shoot ended and apart from its prime function of timber growing the Forestry Commission now concentrates on conservation and recreation. At Salcey it has for some time led the way in this respect. In 1970 it received the Duke of Edinburgh's award for pioneering a nature trail, as a plaque on a stone plinth records, and a variety of forest walks have been created, starting from the picnic area on the road from Hanslope to Quinton, where there are toilets and a large-scale map. In 1986 an Invalid Walk was made, starting from the picnic area, with a surface hard enough to support wheelchairs, and seats at frequent intervals. At the same time a conservation trail with informative markers was instituted at a lay-by a short distance from the B526 at the other side of the forest.

Salcey is an ancient oak forest and so provides a habitat for a variety of wildlife but it is of special interest to naturalists because of the rare butterflies and moths present in favourable surroundings. The county Wildlife Trust has installed bat boxes at six sites to help in the preservation of the declining bat population and the forest also affords a refuge for a great number of wild flowers once common

11

but now largely expunged from the surrounding countryside by intensive farming: violets, primroses, bluebells, ragged-Robin, lady-smocks, wood-sorrel, bugle, herb-Robert and many others appear in their season. In the autumn the dying leaves of beech, oak, maple and other trees give rise to hues that have been compared to those of the New England fall. On the southern (Buckinghamshire) side of Salcey begins Swan's Way, a bridleway running 65 miles (105 km) to end at Goring on Thames, Oxfordshire.

Sywell Country Park, Northampton (OS 152; SP 834650). Telephone: Northampton (0604) 810970. The park is reached from the Earls Barton crossroads on the A4500 road via the minor road to Mears Ashby and Washbrook Lane.

143 acres (50 ha) of parkland surround a 68 acres (28 ha) lake, created around 1900 to provide water for the growing towns of Rushden and Higham Ferrers. The county council bought it in 1983 from Anglia Water, the park being opened in 1985. Below the dam there is an arboretum area with several species of pine trees. A circuit of the lake makes a pleasant walk of 2½ miles (4 km) with changing views caused by the irregular shape of the shore. The shallow arms of the water consist of reed beds and marshland — an ideal habitat for wading birds. There are spacious picnic areas, a visitors' centre and a warden's office. The lake is a good pike and tench fishery and a limited number of day permits are available from the warden.

Titchmarsh Nature Reserve, near Thrapston (OS 141; TL 008805). Leave the A605 2 miles (3 km) north of Thrapston on a track continuing westward from the road to Titchmarsh and park beside the track.

This Northamptonshire Wildlife Trust reserve (opened 1987) is in a gravel pit between the Nene and Harper's Brook and has been landscaped so that small bays, deep-water areas and shallow-water margins provide a variety of habitat, while the seven islands of different sizes give shelter and secure nesting sites for wildfowl, wading birds and common terns. The area of 150 acres (60 ha) is half grassland, some of which will be kept short by sheep and some allowed to grow into long grass with trees and bushes. The Titchmarsh heronry is nearby and those wishing to visit it should contact Lings House (see Lings Wood Nature Trail).

Wakerley Great Wood (OS 141; SP 960988). Forestry Commission. 3 miles (5 km) south of the A43 and A47 road junction.

The Forestry Commission controls more than 6000 acres (2400 ha) of the remains of the great medieval royal hunting forest of Rockingham. This once stretched from Kettering in the south to Stamford in the north. Wakerley Wood has a picnic site, and a waymarked walk of 2½ miles (4 km) around 300 acres (121 ha) of undulating woodland with a great variety of trees. In addition to the usual species of conifers and hardwoods there are Douglas fir, western red cedar and western hemlock. Lime-loving plants abound and six species of fungi, including edible boletus, are present. Both black and red fallow deer live here and during October bucks can be heard 'groaning' during the mating season. Deer have always been plentiful in Rockingham Forest. In 1640 'Venizon brought to Whitehall against Christmas' included 24 from here — the largest contribution from any forest and twice as many as the New Forest provided.

Walking in other places

The Forestry Commission has a number of other woods where people can walk in addition to those mentioned above, although there are no facilities such as toilets. Information about these can be obtained from the following offices: Whittlebury Forest, telephone Silverstone (0327) 857266; Salcey Forest, telephone Yardley Hastings (060 129) 239; Rockingham Forest, telephone Duddington (078 083) 394.

The pamphlet *Out and About in Northamptonshire* has a section 'Waterside places without visitors' facilities', listing those such as the Oxford Canal reservoir at Boddington, where public footpaths give access, and points out that the British Waterways Board allows access also to canal towpaths. It is available from the Leisure and Libraries Department of the county council (27 Guildhall Road, Northampton NN1 1EF). So too is a series of pamphlets detailing walks in the following parishes: Blisworth, Braunston, Bugbrooke, Greatworth, Grendon, Moulton, Nether Heyford, Piddington, Roade, Stoke Bruerne, Weedon Bec and Everdon.

3
Sites of archaeological interest

Apart from four iron age hillforts, the most interesting archaeological sites in Northamptonshire are medieval. The two important castles at Fotheringhay and Northampton have left little trace above ground but earthworks of motte and bailey castles can be seen in a number of places, and along the Northamptonshire uplands depopulated village sites are as thick on the ground as almost anywhere. In 400 square miles (1000 sq km) from north of Badby in the north to Aynho in the south, where there are 113 remaining villages, 29 lost settlements have been recorded. The greatest proportion of these disappeared in the period 1350-1700 as a result mainly of enclosure for sheep farming or the creation of parks attached to country houses. An exception was Elkington, where following the Black Death it was stated that the only surviving parishioners were a few servants at Pipewell Abbey. Only a few typical cases can be listed.

Alderton, near Towcester (OS 152; SP 741469).
The mound of a motte and bailey is adjacent to the church, overlooking the valley of the river Tove, and is covered by trees. It was in use during the reign of Edward I.

Arbury Hill, Badby, near Daventry (OS 152; SP 542586). A public footpath runs from the minor road that goes from Badby to Upper Catesby half a mile (800 metres) west of the A361 and crosses the side of the hill.
Although this is the highest hill in the county at 734 feet (224 metres) it seems less commanding than some because it is surrounded by other hills almost as high, including Blackdown Hill, which is second highest at 727 feet (222 metres) and crowned by a telecommunications tower.
About 400 BC iron age folk occupied a series of hillforts at Arbury Hill, Borough Hill, Hunsbury Hill and Rainsborough Camp, all close to the Jurassic Way (chapter 1). The first-named is roughly square with sides of 600 feet (180 metres) in length and an entrance on the south-west.

Beacon Hill, Wollaston. The village is on the A509, 4 miles (6 km) south of Wellingborough and now bypassed.
Wollaston has a small motte a short distance south of the church and close to the village centre. It is known as Beacon Hill.

Borough Hill, Daventry (OS 152; SP 585625).
Borough Hill is one of the most conspicuous physical features of the county. It stands boldly above the upper reaches of the Nene valley and its 670 foot (198 metre) crest bristles with masts, making it readily identifiable. Its situation made it an ideal site for an iron age fort and its earthworks have been claimed as one of the larger prehistoric fortifications in England. It seems to have been built in two stages, the first on the northern end of the hill, 4½ acres (1.8 ha) in extent; later it took in a further 16 acres (6.5 ha) to the south.
Not only is Borough Hill very visible but it commands far-reaching views, with a panorama thought to be unequalled in the county, including sight of the Wrekin (65 miles, 104 km) and the Chilterns (35 miles, 56 km) when conditions are favourable.
At later dates than the iron age there have been a Roman villa, Anglo-Saxon burials and during the Civil War a Royalist encampment on the hill (chapters 8, 9). Part of the lower slopes are now given over to a golf course, but there are two public rights of way traversing it.

Castle Dykes, near Farthingstone (OS 152; SP 618567). A mile (1.5 km) north of Farthingstone, to the right of the minor road to Weedon Bec.
This is a large motte and bailey earthwork of unusual design. The narrow bailey is almost cut in two by the ringwork of the inner stronghold. There is a large outer bailey and the site is covered by trees.

Castle Yard, Sibbertoft (OS 141; SP 690832).
Up a track a mile (1.5 km) north-east of the village.
This motte and bailey castle stands in the Hothorpe Hills above the Welland valley. It is in a wood and the motte is on the uphill side.

Cliffords Hill, near Little Houghton (OS 152; SP 807605).
A very large motte here closely adjoins the river, as though it was built to control a crossing point. It is remarkable in lacking a bailey and there is no documentary evidence to show why — was it never finished or was it abandoned at an early date because of the collapse of the mound?

Faxton deserted village, near Lamport (OS 141; SP 783753).
Although hardly typical, Faxton is a peculiarly interesting case because its final disappearance has occurred since the Second World War. In the early eighteenth century 32 families lived there and in 1716 a row of four almshouses was built. The 1801 census figure was 54 and it had risen to 108 in 1841. The

Reverend Vere Isham, a member of the Lamport family, started a school there but a decline in numbers led to a 1921 total of 37.

Between the world wars occasional services were held in the church of St Denys by the Reverend W. Watkins-Pitchford, rector of Lamport and father of the well known county author Denys Watkins-Pitchford, but on the outbreak of the Second World War it was closed, never to re-open. After being badly vandalised, the church was demolished in 1959, by which time the village had only one inhabitant. The eleventh-century font went to All Saints' church, Kettering, and the family memorials to the Victoria and Albert Museum.

The boyhood recollections of George Noble, the last person born there, in 1907, the son of a small farmer, record that the environment was such that his mother wanted him to leave home to get away from it, which he did. It appears that others felt the same. Now nothing remains save a memorial marking the site of the church.

Fotheringhay Castle, Fotheringhay (OS 142; TL 062930). 3½ miles (6 km) north of Oundle on the minor road to Wansford.

The remains of the castle are less notable than its history. The picturesque village of Fotheringhay lies between the Nene and its tributary the Willow Brook and this situation must have added to the defensive strength of the castle. Probably originally built by Simon de Senlis, first Earl of Northampton and Huntingdon, it was largely rebuilt by Edward Langley, son of Edward III and founder of the House of York. Leland found it 'fair and meately strong with double ditches and a kepe very ancient and strong' but by the early eighteenth century it was mostly demolished. Richard III was born in the castle but it is chiefly remembered as the last prison and place of execution of Mary, Queen of Scots, who was beheaded there on 8th February 1587 at the age of 44.

All that remains of the stonework is a small section with a plaque attached and fenced off by iron railings, below the massive motte looming over the Nene. Other reminders of the unhappy queen are the gigantic thistles on the site which tradition says she had planted to remind her of Scotland, and Garden Farm, where it is said that Bull, the executioner, stayed in the room over the archway.

The site is privately owned but access is normally allowed in daylight hours. Car parking is on the street nearby.

Hunsbury Hill, Northampton (OS 152; SP 739584).

The rounded shape of Hunsbury dominates Northampton from the south-west (see also chapters 2 and 7). On its top is a small iron age hillfort enclosing 4 acres (1.6 ha) and known locally as Danes Camp because of a fancied Viking connection. Ironstone quarrying began on the hill in 1873 and totally removed the interior of the fort. In succeeding years a rich haul of artefacts showed that generations of iron smelters who occupied the site traded over long distances. Today only the ramparts and ditch of the fort remain. Brooches from Yorkshire decorated with La Tène designs and iron currency bars of the Dobunni tribe in the Forest of Dean suggest that the Jurassic Way which passed here was a trade route (chapter 1). Finds such as these, burnished bowls with incised designs, querns (handmills) and splendid first-century BC sword scabbards are on view in Northampton Central Museum (chapter 6).

Lilbourne (OS 140; SP 551772). The village is squeezed between the M1 and the A5 and is close to the river Avon and the county boundary.

West of the church and traversed by a public footpath is a complex of massive castle earthworks which must have dominated the surrounding countryside, for there appear to have been as many as three mottes.

Muscott deserted village, near Brockhall (OS 152; SP 628634).

On the old Roman road from Duston to Whilton Locks and a mile (1.5 km) short of the latter a very minor road runs down towards the M1. Between this and the gated road to Brockhall going to the left is a 14 acre (6 ha) field full of humps and hollows. In an aerial photograph these show up with great clarity as a village street with house platforms and their crofts behind them. The field is listed as an ancient monument.

Newton in the Willows deserted village, near Geddington (OS 141; SP 884833).

Sometimes a church lingers after the village has gone. The one at Great Newton disappeared along with the village but the chapel of St Faith's at Little Newton stood alone in the fields. In 1958 it was abandoned as a place of worship and was in grave danger when in 1978 it was rescued and adapted for use as a field study centre.

Northampton Castle

Simon de Senlis, the first of three generations of that name who all left their mark on Northampton, was the original builder, beginning in 1084. Few traces remain of what may have been one of the biggest castles ever built, with huge walls along which it was said that six men could walk abreast. Speed's map of 1610 shows outer and inner wards and at least four great towers.

It had many royal connections — being the scene of the confrontation between Henry II and Becket (chapter 10) — and contained two chapels, one for the queen and another for the king. Thirteenth-century documents mention the addition of glass windows. By 1593 Norden wrote of it as 'an eminent castle, ruynous' and following the Civil War the walls were slighted (demolished) because the town had been a Parliamentary stronghold. Materials from it were used in the rebuilding of the town following the great fire of 1675 and its final destruction was brought about when the London and North Western Railway bought the site in 1876 and levelled it to build their station.

A postern gate was rebuilt adjacent to the station entrance but for the rest one must stand on the viewing platform built in Chalk Lane in 1984 and use the plan on the plaque there and one's imagination. The castle lives on in literature, for Shakespeare set the fourth act of *King John* there.

Rainsborough Camp, Charlton-cum-Newbottle, near Brackley (OS 151; SP 526349). A mile south of Charlton-cum-Newbottle and to the west of the minor road leading to Croughton; reached by a footpath which leaves this road a quarter of a mile (400 metres) from Charlton.

This hillfort stands on a plateau at a height of 480 feet (148 metres) above the Cherwell valley and encloses an area of 6¼ acres (2.5 ha). Excavation in 1961-5 showed its history to be long and complicated. In the fifth century BC it was an imposing structure, with an inner rampart of three-tiered wall construction pierced by an entrance with two stone-lined guardhouses at the end of a 60 foot passageway lined with wood, and closed by double gates with a bridge structure over them. Stone walling visible today is the result of eighteenth-century landscape gardening.

Stuchbury deserted village, between Helmdon and Sulgrave (OS 152; SP 564435).

Poll tax figures for 1377 show a village with a population of 59 but other than the name attached to the hall, manor farm and attendant cottages only earthworks and traces of fishponds and footpaths leading to neighbouring villages remain.

4
Churches

Although Northamptonshire is known as the county of 'spires and squires' it must be said that out of more than two hundred medieval churches only about eighty have had spires and some of those, such as Rothwell, no longer exist. Even so, and especially in the Nene valley, these landmarks are very conspicuous. Because of the abundance of good building stone, there is a wealth of fine churches and the following are only a sample.

Ashby St Ledgers: St Leodegarius.
St Leodegarius was bishop of Autun in France and the church with this unusual dedication has a Jacobean two-decker pulpit and a musicians' pew at its west end. The most noteworthy features are the medieval murals, comprising one of the most complete cycles of the Passion of Christ in England with eighteen scenes depicted, although now they are sadly dim. Memorials include a brass to a member of the Catesby family and a monument by Lutyens in the churchyard to the second Lord Wimborne. Both these names are important in the history of the village (chapters 8 and 10).

The church of All Saints, Brixworth.

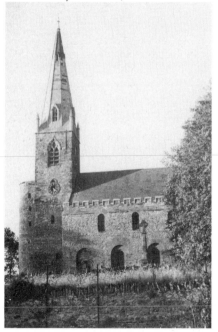

Aynho: St Michael.
The church of St Michael is notable for being an eighteenth-century rebuilding, only the tower of the medieval church remaining. Aynho was for centuries the seat of the Cartwright family so that this south-western projection of the county was known as 'the Cartwright corner'. When Edward Wing designed the new church in 1725 in a style akin to that of Hawksmoor he wrote of 'the pious care, generous encouragement and prudent management' of the contemporary squire of Aynhoe Park.

Barton Seagrave: St Botolph.
The advowson of the church of St Botolph was held by the priory at Kenilworth from the early twelfth century and the monks were responsible for this fine Norman building, which they erected with nave, central tower and chancel. Interior carvings show Norman motifs. In 1724 John Bridges was buried here, long before his great county history, *The History and Antiquities of Northamptonshire,* was published in 1791.

Brigstock: St Andrew.
The church is noted for its Saxon tower of late tenth- or early eleventh-century date. It has typical long and short quoins and a semicircular western extension for a staircase similar to the one at Brixworth. Capped by Decorated work, the spire is also of that period but the nave is Saxon and the north aisle Norman.

Brixworth: All Saints.
Described as 'perhaps the most imposing architectural memorial of the seventh century surviving north of the Alps', this village church is of great importance. In 1980 its thirteen hundredth anniversary was celebrated and, although not as large as formerly, it is still a most imposing structure with a number of remarkable features. It is thought that the stair turret was added in the tenth century, so that although two centuries younger than the main fabric it is also Saxon in origin. At the east end of the church is an apse rebuilt in 1865 on the old foundations and the newest parts, apart from the Victorian work, are the thirteenth-century Lady Chapel on the south side and the fourteenth-century spire. Another notable feature is the presence of Roman tiles in the fabric of arches and parts of the tower.
It seems likely that this noble building arose as an extension of the monastic centre at Medeshamstede (Peterborough), created by monks from Lindisfarne. One of the most

tireless of these northern missionaries was Wilfrid, Bishop of Hexham (chapter 9). There is a theory that he inspired the building of All Saints and since he was a regular visitor to Italy this may be why the shape and dimensions of the church are similar to those of a Roman basilica.

Burton Latimer: St Mary the Virgin.
The church has been much restored externally but is still handsome outside and splendid within. Over the nave arcades are wall paintings of nine of the twelve patriarchs dated about 1600 and on the north wall is a fourteenth-century depiction of the life and martyrdom of St Catherine. There is also a Perpendicular chancel screen, a studded north door made about 1500, a Jacobean chest and poor box and a number of brasses.

Canons Ashby: St Mary.
On the B4525 road from Northampton to Banbury and about 10 miles (16 km) from the latter, the church is seen from some distance in this quiet expanse of the county. It is noteworthy because it is one of only four in England since the Reformation privately owned by the lord of the manor and because the fabric is the only part of a monastic building surviving in the county. Having been disused since about 1951, it was by 1977 at great risk. The Department of the Environment carried out emergency repairs in 1978 and in 1980 the National Trust acquired the church and Canons Ashby House (Chapter 5) and spent a very large sum of money to put them both in good order. This has saved part of the church of a priory of Augustinian canons founded about 1150. It comprises the west end of the nave, which was formerly three times as long, and the fourteenth-century tower, so prominent on the hilltop. Fragmented though it is, there is only one surviving church of the Augustinian order to surpass it — the priory church at Dunstable, Bedfordshire.

Castle Ashby: St Mary Magdalene.
A visitor to the mansion owned by the Marquess of Northampton (chapter 5) might suppose that the church appertains to the great house but it is the parish church and a public path gives access to it. Most of the structure is in the Decorated style and the tower Perpendicular but the north porch has a late Norman doorway embellished by zigzag, lozenges and dogtooth carving, supposedly brought here from a chantry that once existed at Chadstone, about a mile (1.5 km) away. Within the church is a recumbent effigy carved in Purbeck marble of a knight in chain mail. He is thought to have been Sir David de Esseby (of Ashby), who gave his name to the village, which was once known as Ashby David. A notable brass, 5

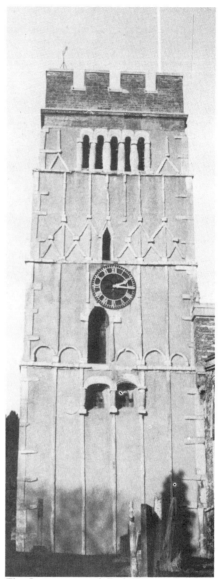

The Saxon tower of Earls Barton church.

feet 3 inches (1.6 metres) long, commemorates William Ermyn, rector (died 1401), and there are a number of memorials to the Compton family, to which the Marquess belongs.

Crick: St Margaret.

St Margaret's is noteworthy in being almost entirely Decorated in style with minimal restoration. The west tower has one of the many fine broach spires found in the county. The circular Norman font is supported by an Italian motif of three kneeling figures and the sedilia and piscina are richly decorated.

Croughton: All Saints.

All Saints' church has some very special murals, including a series of fourteenth-century scenes akin to those found in illuminated manuscripts. On the south wall they trace the story of the life of the Virgin Mary through about twenty episodes and on the north the concluding scenes of Christ's life appear, while over the chancel arch is a fifteenth-century Doom, or Last Judgement.

Daventry: Holy Cross.

The only eighteenth-century church in all the towns of Northamptonshire, it was built in 1752-8. It is an imposing edifice with a distinctive obelisk spire and stands proud above the centre of the old market town.

Denton: St Margaret.

St Margaret's was rebuilt in 1827-8 and the largely blank distempered walls were noticed almost a century later by a boy named Henry Bird. He grew up to be head scenic painter at the Old Vic and Sadler's Wells theatres and then spent years of careful planning and preparation before covering the church walls with paintings. Starting work in 1970, he used local people as models in scenes ancient and modern in this remarkable artistic enterprise.

Dodford: St Mary.

The small village of Dodford and its church nestle in a hollow below the busy A45 road, 3 miles (5 km) from Daventry. Inside the church are a Norman font, a Jacobean pulpit and a splendid assembly of medieval memorials. They include a fourteenth-century effigy of a cross-legged knight, an oak carving of a lady, a tomb chest with another lady with angels by her pillow (thought to be Wentiliana de Keynes, who died in 1376), an alabaster monument to Sir John Cressy dated 1444 and some fifteenth-century brasses.

Earls Barton: All Saints.

The massive 80 foot (24 metre) tower is an archetypal Saxon construction, with some of the stonework suggesting a derivation from timber building. In 1970 visitors came from all over the world to attend the millennium

celebrations. There is also Norman work with zigzag decorations in the south doorway and the arcading of the chancel.

Easton Maudit: St Peter and St Paul.

The church is near the Buckinghamshire border and so is the first of the long line of spires that follows the Nene valley. It is of the most shapely kind — needle-like and recessed with graceful flying buttresses connecting the spire to the pinnacles. The interior of the church has two opulent seventeenth-century monuments of the Yelverton family, who once lived in the now vanished mansion here, and Minton tiles of 1859-60 designed by Lord Alwyne Compton of the Castle Ashby family.

In the years 1753-82 the vicar was the Reverend Thomas Percy and his celebrated *Reliques of Ancient English Poetry* was published from here in 1765. Doctor Samuel Johnson and other literary figures of the age visited him in and in the old vicarage grounds there is still a tract of land known as 'Johnson's Walk'.

Fawsley: St Mary.

St Mary's stands solitary on the edge of parkland overlooking the double lakes created by 'Capability' Brown. The Knightleys have gone from the hall but the church has thirteen monuments to them dating from a brass of 1516 to a memorial of 1856. Most notable is an alabaster tomb chest flanked by the figures of the four daughters and eight sons of Sir Richard and his wife (1534).

Fotheringhay: St Mary and All Saints.

Edmund Langley, founder of the House of York, began to build a college attached to the church about 1370 and the work was continued by his son Edward of York, so that the college was founded in 1411. It comprised a master, twelve fellows, eight clerks and thirteen choristers and as at that time the castle was probably at its strongest Fotheringhay must have looked quite different from today. At the Dissolution of the monasteries the grand chancel and the college buildings were pulled down so that what remains is truncated, though still splendid. The graceful octagonal lantern tower shines over the Nene water-meadows and inside there is a feeling of light and air despite the tragedies that attended the York family.

When Queen Elizabeth I visited she found the graves of her Plantagenet ancestors — Edward, who fell at Agincourt, and Richard, killed at Wakefield — in disarray and ordered the building of identical and imposing monuments in 1573. Also buried in the church is Cicely Neville, wife of Richard and mother of

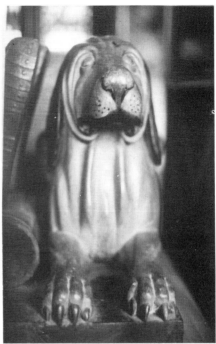

(Left) *The church of St Mary and All Saints, Fotheringhay.*
(Right) *The hound on a Spencer tomb at Great Brington.*

Edward IV. The latter brought back the bodies of his father and brother Edmund, both killed at Wakefield, to Fotheringhay.

Great Brington: St Mary.
Just as monuments at Fawsley recall the history of the Knightley family so does the Spencer Chapel at St Mary's recall that of the Spencer family of Althorp. Nine major memorials range from 1522 to 1833 and include work by Hollemans, Nicholas Stone, Nollekens, Flaxman and Chantrey. The ironstone church stands on a knoll near the edge of Althorp Park and a wide prospect spreads to the north of it.

Higham Ferrers: St Mary.
Whichever way you approach Higham, the thirteenth-century spire of St Mary's soaring to 170 feet (52 metres) stands out. The church is one part of an ecclesiastical complex (chapter 10) but would be magnificent if it stood alone. Its style has been compared with that of Westminster Abbey and there are two remarkable west doorways which have affinities with French cathedrals because of their elaborate carvings showing scenes from the life of Christ. The interior of the church is equally outstand-ing with fourteenth-century work that includes a north aisle as wide as the nave and continuing in a Lady Chapel as spacious as the chancel. Twenty of the stalls remain from Archbishop Chichele's foundation with misericords, including his portrait and the Chichele arms. A wealth of brasses is to be found in the Lady Chapel and one attached to a tomb chest between the chapel and the chancel is among the best in England. It does not belong to the tomb chest. Dated 1337, it represents a priest, Laurence St Maur, and is 5 feet 4 inches (1.63 metres) long.

Irthlingborough: St Peter.
There are some parallels between St Peter's and the church at Fotheringhay. Both had medieval colleges attached to them — that at Irthlingborough was founded in 1388 by the widow of John Pyel, a London mercer — and both have prominent octagonal towers, but that at Irthlingborough rises above a small industrial town. There are some remains of the widow Pyel's college in the form of two undercrofts with rib vaults.

Kettering: Fuller Baptist Church, Gold Street.
Kettering, in common with much of the

19

county, was a stronghold of nonconformity and the Baptist church was founded in 1696. The present building was built in 1861-2 by Sharman of Wellingborough for Sir Morton Peto, the great Victorian railway contractor. It has a late classical ashlar facade and a round-arched one-storey portico.

Kettering: St Peter and St Paul.
Most of the building is Perpendicular. The crocketed spire is of the most elegant recessed kind and rises to 179 feet (55 metres). It shows to great advantage, being set back from the main road and approached along an avenue of trees. The tower is built of Barnack stone distinctly darker than the spire and contains a unique peal of twelve bells. Inside the church there is a fine parish chest containing a mass of records going back to 1637, and also a brass to Edmund Sawyer, who probably erected the south or Sawyer's Aisle early in the seventeenth century and whose family built Sawyer's Hospital, now known as the Alms-houses, in 1688.

Kings Sutton: St Peter and St Paul.
The church is at the extreme south-west corner of the county, about as far as one can get from the Nene valley within the borders of Northamptonshire. Yet it has one of the tallest spires (198 feet, 60 metres) and possibly the finest of them all. Recessed and crocketed, it is the church's crowning glory. The church itself is an intriguing mixture of styles and contains a Norman font and a screen by Sir George Gilbert Scott, who restored the building in 1866 and has other connections with the county.

Lowick: St Peter.
St Peter's, one of only a few Perpendicular churches in the county, occupies a most commanding situation in its locality. It has a tower with an octagonal lantern similar to that at Fotheringhay and it was built chiefly by three members of the Greene family of Drayton. Sir Henry, who along with Bushy and Bagot was executed in 1399, was followed by Ralph and another Henry. The last had to do with the building of the tower, which was completed some time after his death in 1467-8. A contract of 1415 exists for the tomb of Sir Ralph made with Thomas Prentys and Robert Sutton, 'Kervers of Chellaston', the Derby-shire village with alabaster quarries, to make images of an esquire and a lady, holding hands, with angels beside them and dogs at their feet. All this can still be seen.

Middleton Cheney: All Saints.
Like its neighbour at Kings Sutton, All Saints' has a spire which is a very conspicuous feature in the valley of the river Cherwell but the main attraction is not the architecture but the stained glass windows. In 1864 the incumbent was the Reverend W. Buckley, a friend of Edward Burne-Jones, and the firm of William Morris has left a splendid set of windows to which Burne-Jones and other Pre-Raphaelite painters, including Philip Webb and Ford Madox Brown, contributed. The work continued until 1892, when two north windows in the chancel were created by Burne-Jones as a memorial to Buckley, who died in that year.

Northampton: All Saints.
In the late seventeenth century All Saints' church, which dominates the centre of the town, was described as one of the stateliest of its date outside London. This was after its rebuilding following the great fire of 1675, when it was burnt down save for the base of the west tower. Large as the present structure is, the medieval church was almost twice as long. The pillared portico carries a somewhat strange statue of Charles II, wearing a wig and a Roman toga. This was installed because after the fire he gave a thousand tons of timber from local forests to help with the rebuilding of the town. On 29th May (Oakapple Day) it is customary for the verger to climb up to the statue and adorn it with a garland of oak leaves.

Northampton: Holy Sepulchre, Sheep Street.
'Saint Seps', as it is known to local people is a great rarity: a round church that has always been a parish church. Like the castle, it was orginally built by the first Simon de Senlis following his return from the First Crusade and it recalls the rotunda forming part of the church of the same name in Jerusalem. In 1116 Simon handed over the church to the monks of the Cluniac priory of St Andrew which he had helped to found and it remained in their hands until the Dissolution. The early fourteenth-century recessed spire is a noticeable landmark and the whole east end of the church was built by Sir George Gilbert Scott in 1860-4.

Northampton: St Benedict, Hunsbury.
The new church with its unusually shaped tower stands high on Hunsbury Hill, where it serves the southern district of greater North-ampton. It may not look like other towers of earlier date but it does hold a ring of bells, all new and called after saints, including St Ragener, nephew of St Edmund and a local Saxon martyr.

Northampton: St Giles.
The church gives its name to the important street where it stands and, dedicated to the patron saint of cripples and beggars, was outside the town walls when built but was taken in during the fourteenth century when

The church of St Peter, Lowick.

the fortifications were extended to the east. The Norman tower fell in 1613 and the upper parts were rebuilt then and again in 1914. The west doorway is also Norman but restored and reset when the church was lengthened.

Outside the south front is a monument to Robert Browne (about 1550 to about 1633), a most turbulent priest and founder of the sect called the Brownists, forerunners of the Independents, or Congregationalists. When over eighty, he was brought in his bed on a cart to Northampton jail, where he died. It was a fitting place to meet his end because Northampton was always a breeding ground for nonconformity (chapter 10).

Northampton: St John the Baptist, Bridge Street.

Of all the many religious houses in the town only St John's Hospital survives. It now functions as a Roman Catholic church. Founded by William de Saint Clare about 1138, the original infirmary hall later became an almshouse but the chapel remained. The Roman Catholic church bought the buildings in 1877 and the inmates were transferred to a new institution at Weston Favell.

Northampton: St Matthew, Kettering Road.

This was one of a number of churches erected as part of the town's Victorian expansion. Designed by Matthew Holding, an architect very busy in Northampton at that time, it was built in the early 1890s and the 170 foot (52 metre) spire was irreverently known as 'Phipps's fire escape', because a member of a well known local brewing family paid for it. The church is notable because of the artistic acquisitions made by Canon Hussey, who went on to become Dean of Chichester. In 1944 he commissioned Henry Moore's Madonna, sculpted in Horton stone, and soon after Graham Sutherland's painting of the Crucifixion.

Northampton: St Peter, Marefair.

This is in the oldest part of the town not far from where the castle stood. Excavation suggests that the site was at the centre of the Middle Saxon settlement of 20-25 acres (8-10 ha) and that a church of about AD 700 was near the present site. The present building is twelfth-century and typically Norman, having been built possibly by Simon de Senlis II, and gives an impression of massive solidity, quite unmoved by the heavy motor traffic along the dual carriageway below, called St Peter's Way.

The interior has features more akin to cathedrals such as Durham and Peterborough than to an ordinary parish church and there is much ornate decoration such as zigzags and lozenges. Among many monuments are those to William Smith (1769-1839), who founded the science of modern geology, and to George Baker and his sister, who lived in Hazelrigg House (chapter 10). Between 1823 and 1841 George Baker wrote the second great history

21

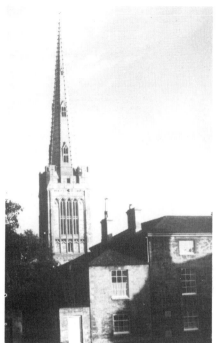

The church of St Peter, Oundle.

of the county, *History and Antiquities of Northamptonshire*, in two volumes, and although incomplete, it is a mine of information.

Northampton: nonconformist churches.

There are many of these in the town but the most historically significant is the Doddridge Street United Reform (formerly Congregational) Church, Castle Hill. The name of the street derives from the great preacher and hymn writer Philip Doddridge DD (1702-51), who for 22 years was minister to the Castle Hill Meeting. The square stone building was built in 1695, enlarged in 1862, and has a pyramid roof.

Grander in appearance is the College Street Baptist church of 1863, which has large columns supporting a pediment. A building formerly belonging to the chapel is now a small shopping precinct.

Oundle: St Peter.

The church of St Peter is the most noticeable feature of this small and picturesque town because of its tall, slender Decorated tower and elegant needle-like spire. Most of the church is thirteenth-century but the south porch, built about 1485, is Perpendicular.

Inside there is a noble fifteenth-century lectern in the shape of a brass eagle, similar to those found at Southwell Minster, Nottinghamshire, and Newcastle upon Tyne Cathedral, and a brass chandelier dated 1685.

Passenham: St Guthlac.

The unusual dedication to St Guthlac refers to a Mercian nobleman who became a hermit in the wastes of the vast fen that existed in the seventh century between Mercia and East Anglia (what is now Northamptonshire being then in Mercia). After his death in AD 714 his shrine became the nucleus of the great abbey at Crowland, Lincolnshire.

The most striking feature of the church is the 'faire chauncel' created by Sir Robert Banastre in the 1620s. Its wall paintings caused a sensation when they were uncovered and restored in the years 1956-66. The ceiling was repainted blue with gold stars so that the whole effect resembled its original state. A bust of Sir Robert gazes benignly on his creation but he left a legacy of superstition in the neighbourhood (chapter 9).

Raunds: St Mary.

St Mary's church has an Early English broach spire in the Nene valley series and it is one of the most shapely of its kind. Its size and opulence are indications of the successful thirteenth-century exploitation of arable cultivation in the region. On the church is a fifteenth-century clock dial held in place by two angels, behind whom kneel the donors, John Elen and his wife. Also dating from the thirteenth century is the elaborate six-light east window and within the church there are a Jacobean communion rail, fifteenth-century wall paintings and brasses and an eighteenth-century brass chandelier.

Rothwell: Holy Trinity.

Holy Trinity is best known for its macabre charnel house or bone crypt but it has many other more agreeable features. At 173 feet (53 metres) it is the longest church in the county and yet it shows signs of having been even larger. Its spire was removed after being struck by lightning in 1660. It has kept thirteenth-century sedilia and a piscina, a five-light east window, stalls with poppy-heads and a number of brasses, including one of William de Rothwell, archdeacon, who died in 1361. Sir Adrian Boult said that the acoustics were better than any concert hall in Europe and many leading orchestras have played here.

Rushden: St Mary.

For the most part a very splendid Perpendicular church, St Mary's has a recessed crocketed spire 164 feet (50 metres) high, one of the many fine examples along the Nene valley. Its outstanding internal feature is a great strainer arch across the nave with intricate tracery and other elegant embellishments.

Stowe-Nine-Churches: St James the Great.
Upper Stowe is separated from Church Stowe by a deep dell. The Victorian church of St James the Great at Upper Stowe was built in 1855 at the behest of the incumbent, the Reverend Henry Crawley, who served the parish in the years 1849-95. A member of a well known clerical family who were leaders of the Oxford Movement, he rode the local lanes on a 'stout cob' distributing 'Tracts for the Times', the pamphlets by which the Movement disseminated its ideas.

Stowe-Nine-Churches: St Michael.
St Michael's at Church Stowe stands proud on a hilltop overlooking the upper reaches of the Nene valley. This situation and the odd name of the parish, which comprises both Church and Upper Stowe, have given rise to one of the county's best known legends (chapter 9). There has been much discussion as to whether the tall Saxon tower is leaning. The chief interest is within the church. Here are some notable monuments, including a Purbeck marble effigy of a knight said to represent Sir Gerard de l'Isle (1287), Elizabeth, Lady Carey, carved in white marble by Nicholas Stone about 1620, and an imposing standing monument to Doctor Thomas Turner, President of Corpus Christi, Oxford (1714).

Towcester: St Laurence.
The ironstone church is secluded from the busy A5 in Church Lane. The name of Archdeacon Sponne, rector in the years 1422-48, is well known in the town (chapter 10). There is a gruesome reminder of him in the church, where his memorial consists of an effigy above a realistic cadaver.

Warkton (St Edmund) and **Weekley** (St Mary).
Both these churches are within the Boughton estate and so contain impressive monuments of the Montagu family. At Weekley are those to Sir Edward Montagu, Chief Justice of the King's Bench (1557), and two Sir Edward Montagus, (1602 and 1664). The chancel at Warkton was built about 1750 to receive four monuments. Among them are two of Roubiliac's finest works: John, Duke of Montagu (1752), and Mary, Duchess of Montagu (1753).

Wellingborough: All Hallows.
The town has grown and is a very busy place but All Hallows, the parish church, is removed from the traffic and as the churchyard is well treed the atmosphere is calm. There is a

Norman south doorway, a thirteenth-century tower with a later broach spire with pinnacles, and a Decorated chancel with a spectacular five-light window. Six stalls with misericords form an interesting series showing a wood carver, an alewife with customer, a mermaid, an eagle, two lions, a fox and a goose. Two uncommon modern features are a wall painting of 1952 in the south transept and a stained glass window of 1955 in the east window of the south aisle.

Wellingborough: St Mary, Knox Road.
This church has been judged the most complete achievement of Sir Ninian Comper. Beginning with the north chapel in 1908, it grew stage by stage until the nave was reached in 1930. The interior is brilliantly and lavishly furnished in the 'High Church' fashion for which the architect was noted.

Wellingborough: nonconformist churches.
The United Reform Church (formerly Congregationalist) in the High Street is said to be unique — it has an egg-shaped plan — and has been described as the most successful experiment in free church architecture in the county. The Friends' Meeting House in St John Street is a very pleasant small ironstone building of 1819 with arched windows.

Whiston: St Mary.
St Mary's stands isolated on a hilltop above the Nene valley and can be reached only on foot. It is remarkable because it was built by one man to a unified design unaltered to this day. Anthony Catesby was a descendant of the Ashby St Ledgers family and created the church over a period of more than twenty years early in the sixteenth century. The church is topped by a tower having brown and grey ashlar courses and in style and size worthy to rank with those of Somerset.

De-consecrated churches.
In addition to All Saints' at Aldwincle (chapter 8) two other churches have been de-consecrated and put to other use with happy results.
The former chapel of St Faith's at Little Newton, near Geddington, is the remnant of a deserted village site and stood alone in the fields (chapter 3). In 1958 it was abandoned as a place of worship and was in grave danger when in 1978 it was rescued and adapted for use as a field study centre. Nearby is a dovecote reputedly the largest in England — a relic of a Tresham family mansion that has also disappeared.
What was once the church of All Saints at Orton, 4 miles (6 km) west of Kettering, has been converted into a training centre for stonemasons by the Orton Trust.

Boughton House, Kettering.

5
Historic buildings and gardens

Morton remarked early in the eighteenth century that the county has 'no naked and craggy rocks, no rugged and unsightly mountains' and the lack of barren ground was a great recommendation to landowners. In Elizabethan times Norden said that Northamptonshire was 'adorned with salutarie and profitable seates' and 'so plentifullie stored with gentry in regard whearof this shire may seeme worthy to be termed the Heralds Garden'.

To this day the Duke of Buccleuch at Boughton, the Marquess of Northampton at Castle Ashby, Earl Spencer at Althorp, Lord Hesketh at Easton Neston and the Brudenells of Deene (once Earls of Cardigan) still remain. Although others have gone, their mansions still grace the landscape and in most cases can be visited by the public, although some of the places described here are open only occasionally and intending visitors should always find out opening dates and hours before making a special journey.

Althorp, Northampton NN7 4HG. Telephone: Northampton (0604) 770209. 6 miles (10 km) north-west of Northampton off the A428.

Long before Diana, the youngest daughter of the eighth Earl Spencer, became Princess of Wales the Spencer family had a distinguished history. The first Lord Spencer engaged Ben Jonson to write a masque performed before James I's queen, Anne of Denmark. A later member of the family became Duke of Marlborough (hence Winston S. Churchill's second name) and a Viscount Althorp was leader of the House of Commons and piloted the Reform Bill of 1832. He was known as 'Honest Jack' — an appellation not accorded to many politicians. The fifth Earl was known as the 'Red Earl' because of a long red beard which enhanced an imposing presence and was in late Victorian times twice Lord Lieutenant of Ireland and later First Lord of the Admiralty.

The Spencer fortunes were founded on wool and this enabled John Spencer in 1513 to empark 440 acres (178 ha) at Althorp, where a medieval moated house stood. Sixty years later another John Spencer enlarged the house, adding extensive wings and concealing the stone and half-timbered work beneath red brick. From 1660 onward André le Nôtre, the gardener of Versailles, was employed to design the avenues and the oval lake. The second Earl Spencer commissioned Henry Holland to alter the house drastically both within and without in the years 1789-91 and he gave it something like its present appearance.

The entrance hall is reckoned the most noble Georgian room in the county and the great staircase which fills the space of a former courtyard is breathtaking in its size. The grandeur of the house is equalled by the splendour of the furniture and paintings. The latter include portraits by Van Dyck, Lely, Kneller, Gainsborough, Hoppner, Orpen, Sir

William Nicholson, Augustus John and a whole collection by Sir Joshua Reynolds.

Aynhoe Park, Aynho, near Banbury OX17 3BQ. Telephone: Croughton (0869) 810636. 6 miles (10 km) south-east of Banbury on the A41.

From 1615 on this was the seat of the Cartwright family. Their original manor house was set on fire in 1645 by Royalist troops and the present building contains work of the Carolean period and the early eighteenth century, with later additions by Sir John Soane. The 'handsome stone building of two fronts', as it was described in Victorian times, remains but the Cartwrights have departed. The house now belongs to the Country Houses Association, which provides unfurnished apartments for retired people.

Barnwell Castle, near Oundle. Off the A605 3 miles (5 km) south of Oundle.

HRH the Duke of Gloucester opens the grounds of the castle twice a year as advertised in local papers. The dates can also be obtained from Oundle tourist information centre (chapter 12).

Barnwell is remarkable for the juxtaposition of the house and the shell of the ancient castle. Before the Dissolution of the monasteries the castle belonged to the abbey of Peterborough, but it was sold to Sir Edward Montagu, who built a new dwelling in the outer courtyard. It has been much added to since, including work in 1913 and later. Architecturally, the chief interest is in the castle, which Pevsner thought might have been built by Berenger Le Moyne about 1266 and so could be the prototype of the sort of castle building found at Harlech, Gwynedd. It has a square plan and round corner towers. A gatehouse on the east side has two round towers. The flat site by the Nene makes it less impressive than some but it foreshadows the Edwardian castles of North Wales.

Boughton House, Kettering NN14 1BJ. Telephone: Kettering (0536) 515731. 3 miles (5 km) north of Kettering on the A43.

The Northamptonshire home of the Montagu-Douglas-Scott family is the centre of an estate of 11,000 acres (4500 ha) and the biggest country house in the county. Sir Edward Montagu, Lord Chief Justice to Henry VIII, bought the monastery that stood here in 1528 and built a manor house with courtyards on to the monks' great hall. Further wings and courts were added and finally in the 1690s the spectacular north front — including entrance halls, state rooms and stables — was created to complete a building that has had no further structural alteration, so that it appears today as it was then. Ralph, first Duke of Montagu,

who had been ambassador in Paris and loved French architecture, had the facade designed to resemble a French *château* but behind lies a mass of typically English building.

Furniture and paintings are sumptuous and the latter include works by Murillo, David Teniers the younger, Zucchero, Van Dyck, Lely, El Greco and many others. The walls and ceiling of the staircase, the hall and the ceilings of the Egyptian Hall and Great Hall were painted for Duke Ralph by Louis Chéron. Much of the furniture is also French. The first Duke bought and ran the Mortlake Tapestry Factory (1674-91) and several examples of the craft adorn the walls.

His son was known as 'John the Planter' because of his zeal in creating avenues once totalling 70 miles (113 km) in length. The elms have gone but the limes survive in good shape.

Pamphlets are provided so that trails can be followed in the 350 acre (140 ha) park. In 1985 the Living Landscape Trust was founded to provide a centre where people with an interest in and a concern for rural matters can see, hear and discuss all the aspects of a working estate where farming, forestry, game rearing, conservation and leisure amenities are all catered for.

Canons Ashby House, Canons Ashby, Daventry NN11 6SD. Telephone: Blakesley (0327) 860044. National Trust. 14 miles (22 km) south-west of Northampton on the B4525 road to Banbury.

Like St Mary's church (chapter 4), the former seat of the Drydens (the family of the poet) was at risk until the National Trust took over in 1980. The architecture belongs to three stages from the sixteenth century to the eighteenth and since the early nineteenth century has not changed. One of its most striking features is the pele tower, which is explained by the Drydens' Cumbrian connection.

The gardens are also of special interest. They have been resurrected from a state of wilderness and are a rare and valuable survival from the early eighteenth century. The axial arrangement of paths and terraces, high stone walls and ornamental gateways is a classical example of the fashion of that period and the plants are contemporary with it.

Castle Ashby House, Castle Ashby, near Northampton NN7 1LQ. Telephone: Yardley Hastings (060 129) 234. Off the A428 Bedford road 9 miles (15 km) east of Northampton. Open by appointment for groups of twenty plus, on special occasions only.

The mansion stands four-square at the end of an avenue 3½ miles (6 km) long and was built between 1574 and 1640. A remarkable feature is the giant lettering in Latin around

Castle Ashby House, near Northampton.

the parapet of the words of the 127th psalm (in English: 'Except the Lord build the house ...'). *Nisi Dominus*, the opening words in Latin, is the motto of the Compton family, who were at Compton Wynyates from early in the thirteenth century before building Castle Ashby House on or near the site of the medieval castle which gave the place its name.

Within the house is the Great Hall, where concerts are often held. There is an early seventeeth-century plaster ceiling in King William's Dining Room, created by James Leigh, Master Plasterer to James I (the name arose because William III used the room in 1695). There are Brussels and Mortlake tapestries, furniture of most periods including splendid chinoiserie and paintings by Italian old masters and family portraits by William Dobson, Kneller, Benjamin West, Reynolds, Raeburn and others.

The 200 acre (80 ha) parkland is thought to be some of the finest in England and when 'Capability' Brown created the series of ponds he stood on his Terracotta Bridge and declaimed: 'Thames, Thames, thou wilt never forgive me!' The mansion, with its east and north terraces designed by Matthew Digby Wyatt in Victorian times, the orangery and Italian garden also created by him, the nearby church and the South Avenue make an ensemble it would be difficult to excel. The gardens are almost always open and there is a delightful circular walk beside lakes and round the arboretum, where in spring bulbs bloom in profusion.

Compton Estates have created other walks and a picnic area beside the lakes along the road to Grendon and coarse fishing is available there in season.

Deene Park, Deene, Corby NN17 3EW. Telephone: Bulwick (078 085) 361. On the western side of the A43 road 6 miles (10 km) north-east of Corby.

The Brudenells had already lived in the county for 250 years when Sir Robert, later Chief Justice of Common Pleas, bought Deene in 1514. The title of Earl of Cardigan was held by the family from 1661 until the death of the seventh and most famous of the line, who led the Charge of the Light Brigade and gave his name to a very useful woollen garment.

Little remains of the original medieval house but there is a great hall, completed about 1570 by Sir Robert's grandson Edmund, which has a lofty hammerbeam roof and contains an Elizabethan refectory table and bench. The third Earl improved the garden, adding a lake and a stone bridge, and the seventh Earl added the octagonal summerhouse so that he could entertain ladies uninterrupted, since people approaching were visible at a distance from the upstairs room.

The house centres on a courtyard and is still very much a family home, containing fine examples of period furniture. There are many family portraits and paintings of all Lord Cardigan's hunters by John Ferneley, along with one of him galloping to the attack on his charger Ronald. Elsewhere his uniforms and the head and tail of Ronald are displayed.

Delapre Abbey, London Road, Northampton NN4 9AW. Telephone: Northampton (0604) 762129.

The abbey, one of only two Cluniac nunneries in England, was founded by the second Simon de Saint Liz or Senlis about 1145 and took its name from the water-meadows of the river Nene — *de la pré* — in which it was situated. The present building stands on this site — there is little of the nunnery remaining — and mostly dates from the time of Zouch Tate (1617-51), a member of the family who acquired the property after the Dissolution. The south facade and stables are mid eighteenth-century additions.

The Bouverie family were the last to occupy it as a home. It was sold after the Second World War to Northampton Borough Council

and by the 1950s it was in a dilapidated condition and on the verge of being pulled down. This was prevented by the intervention of Miss Joan Wake, founder of the Northamptonshire Record Society in 1920, who was concerned to maintain the documentary heritage of the county. She mobilised both money and public opinion so that Delapre could be opened as the home of the Record Office in 1958 and it stands as a fitting memorial to her great spirit.

Near the house is a walled herb garden, a 'wilderness' garden and a public park.

Edgcote House, near Banbury OX17 1AG. Telephone: Chipping Warden (029 586) 257. 1 mile (1.5 km) east of the A361 road 6 miles (10 km) north-east of Banbury. Open by appointment only.

The house is in the upper reaches of the Cherwell valley in what was described in Victorian times as 'a delightfully secluded situation' and it still is so today. Built in the mid eighteenth century for the Chauncey family, along with the tree-girt medieval church it forms a harmonious whole. The house cost £20,000 to build and the names of the craftsmen who carried out the work in masonry, woodwork and so on are still known. The Chaunceys are also remembered by a series of monuments in the church which date from 1579, including four by Rysbrack.

Deene Park, Corby.

27

The Geddington (left) and Hardingstone Crosses were erected to commemorate the stopping places of the body of Eleanor, wife of Edward I.

Eleanor Crosses, Geddington and Hardingstone.

When Queen Eleanor, wife of Edward I, died near Lincoln in 1290 her embalmed body was carried to London for burial in Westminster Abbey. At stopping places at the end of each day during the journey south Eleanor Cross memorials were built and of the three that survive two are in Northamptonshire.

The one at Geddington is the most complete. The reason for the halt there was presumably because there was a royal hunting lodge in the village and Edward I was there in 1274, 1275 and 1279 (chapter 10). The cross remains today as a marvellous centrepiece to the village, surrounded by stone dwellings and adjacent to the picturesque Star Inn.

The location of the Hardingstone cross is more dramatic, for it stands high on a bank near the crest of the long hill where the London road climbs out of Northampton. The road runs alongside Delapre Park, where once stood the nunnery at which the queen's body rested. The cross is octagonal and three-tiered but lacks the crowning terminal. This may

have been broken as early as 1460, for a description of the battle of Northampton of that date speaks of the 'headless' cross, saying that the Archbishop of Canterbury and the Papal Legate watched the struggle from beside it. It was restored in the early 1980s and now stands proud and pristine despite great age.

Holdenby House and Gardens, near East Haddon, Northampton NN6 8DJ. Telephone: Northampton (0604) 770241 and 770786.

'Holmby', as it is locally said, stands in a tract of rolling 'shire' country midway between the A50 and A428 roads 7 miles (11 km) north-west of Northampton.

Late in the sixteenth century there stood on this site the largest house in England, built by Sir Christopher Hatton, Lord Chancellor to Elizabeth I. Norden said of it: 'the state of the same House is such, and so beautiful, that it may well delight a Prince'. James I must have thought this, for he bought it in 1607, but his son, Charles I, was imprisoned there for four months in 1647. On 4th June in that year Cornet Joyce came to take the King into the custody of the army. When Charles asked what commission he had to do this Joyce pointed to the well armed troop of cavalry waiting between the two base court arches — one fragment of Hatton's palace that remains. 'There, Sire, is my commission', he said, to which the King drily replied ''Tis well writ' and left with his captors.

Soon after the Civil War the house was sold and most of it torn down, leaving only the arches and the kitchen wing. The latter formed the basis of the Victorian rebuilding to its present form. This looks substantial but Hatton's establishment was eight times as large.

The gardens have much to offer. Not only can the vestigial outlines of the huge Elizabethan garden be traced also, but an Elizabethan flower plot has been re-created and there are other horticultural features.

In 1985 Holdenby won the Sandford Award for its imaginative educational programme and projects on offer to school parties. There are rare breeds of farm animals on display, a 'cuddle farm' and donkey rides for children, a pottery museum, a falconry centre and a church.

Kelmarsh Hall, Kelmarsh NN6 9LY. Telephone: Maidwell (060 128) 276. On the A508 11 miles (18 km) north of Northampton. Entrance by the South Lodge at the Kelmarsh crossroads.

The hall stands in rolling country and was once used by a keen follower of hounds so that in a lobby there is a large hand-painted map of the Pytchley country.

Kelmarsh is one of the finest of the smaller stately homes in Northamptonshire. It is an architectural entity, because in the 1950s Victorian accretions were removed and the house was restored to something very close to what James Gibbs planned when it was built about 1727-32. The mellow red brick and balanced Palladian design with symmetrical wings are most pleasing and although Gibbs was the architect for many famous buildings, including the church of St Martin in the Fields, London, Kelmarsh is one of only two of his country houses surviving today.

In 1778 James Wyatt designed lodge gates which were not then built. The drawings were found in Northampton Public Library and the south gates finally erected in the 1960s.

The charming gardens lead from one point of interest to another through topiary and shrubberies. From them are visible in the park the herd of British White cattle like those at Chillingham.

Kirby Hall, Deene, near Corby NN17 3EN. Telephone: Corby (0536) 3230. English Heritage.

The remains of this great house ranged round its courtyards — so well preserved that it seems almost as though it were half-built rather than half-ruined — are of much importance to students of Elizabethan architecture and are very impressive. It was built originally for Sir Humphrey Stafford (the Stafford knot is in evidence) and after his death the work was carried on by Sir Christopher Hatton simultaneously with that at Holdenby.

The formal gardens laid out about 1685 have been reconstructed since the late 1960s and form an interesting adjunct to the ruins of the great mansion.

Kirby Hall, near Corby.
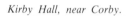

Lamport Hall, Lamport, Northampton NN6 9HD. Telephone: Maidwell (060 128) 272. Off the A508 9 miles (15 km) north of Northampton.

Until his death in 1976 this was the home of Sir Gyles Isham, twelfth Baronet, the last resident squire of a long line of Ishams, for they were here from 1560 onwards. The early design of the hall was by John Webb, pupil of Inigo Jones, and later Francis and William Smith added wings to the original *palazzo* but kept the Palladian style.

The gardens have wooded and alpine sections, a picnic area and nature trail. Sir Charles Isham, a Victorian eccentric, brought what are thought to have been the first garden gnomes to Britain from Germany. Only one survives but an attempt is being made to reconstruct his famous rock garden on which the gnomes were displayed.

Cultural events at Lamport include musical concerts, craft fairs, antique exhibitions, country fairs and seminars.

Lyveden New Bield, Oundle. Telephone: Benefield (083 25) 358. National Trust. 4 miles (7 km) south-west of Oundle via the A427, then along the Harley Way from Oundle to Brigstock and finally up a rough track.

The New Bield is one of a number of strange edifices built by Sir Thomas Tresham, mostly in Elizabethan days, but this dates to 1604-5. The New Bield (building) was designed as a lodge or summerhouse to the Manor House, or Old Building, at Lyveden. Like the

Triangular Lodge at Rushton (see below), it shows a recusant's fixation with religious symbols in its cruciform shape and elaborate sculptured decoration and lettering, though it is now a roofless ruin.

Priest's House, Easton-on-the-Hill, near Stamford. Telephone: Stamford (0780) 62506. National Trust. Open by appointment with Mr R. Chapman, Glebe Cottage, 45 West Street, Easton-on-the-Hill. The key can be obtained from key holders listed on the building.

Dating back to the late fifteenth century, this is one of the few priest's houses in Britain surviving from the middle ages. It now contains a collection of village bygones.

Rockingham Castle, Rockingham, near Market Harborough LE16 8TH. Telephone: Rockingham (0536) 770240. Rockingham is on the A6003 a mile (1.5 km) north of the edge of Corby.

The castle was originally built by William the Conqueror in a dominating situation on the scarp above the Welland valley. The village is at the foot of the hill. The gatehouse with twin drum towers survives from the medieval fortifications and was used in the television historical drama *By the Sword Divided,* set in the time of the Civil War. Sir Lewis Watson, who owned Rockingham Castle at that time, suffered from both sides. First the castle was bombarded by the artillery of Fairfax and stormed by the Roundheads and then King Charles was so displeased at its loss

Lamport Hall, Northampton.

The Lyveden New Bield, Oundle.

that Sir Lewis was imprisoned at Belvoir Castle.

There are many notable paintings in the castle, including work by Van Dyck, Reynolds, Zoffany and Constable and a number of more modern works by Stanley Spencer and his contemporaries. There are also some by the sporting artist Ben Marshall, a *protégé* of the Watson family crippled in 1819 in a coaching accident on the hill at Rockingham.

A frequent visitor to the castle from 1846 on was Charles Dickens, who dedicated *David Copperfield* to his friends Richard and Lavinia Watson and used the place in his description of Chesney Wold, the home of Lady Dedlock in *Bleak House*.

Southwick Hall, Peterborough PE8 5BL. Telephone: Oundle (0832) 74064. Beside a minor road 3 miles (5 km) north-west of Oundle on the way to Woodnewton.

The hall retains two stair turrets and adjoining rooms from the medieval house built by the Knyvett family, Sir John Knyvett being Lord Chancellor to Edward III. The south wing was built in the reign of Elizabeth I on the foundations of the medieval hall. Further additions were made in mid eighteenth century and in the nineteenth, when George Capron, the great great grandfather of the present owner, added the stable block and rebuilt the east wing. So the house illustrates the gradual development of a manor house and remains today a family home. It contains, amid much

else, a Victorian and Edwardian exhibition and collection of carpentry and rural tools.

Stoke Park Pavilions, Stoke Bruerne NN12 7RZ. Telephone: Roade (0604) 862172. Off the A508, turn off the minor road from Stoke Bruerne to Shutlanger down the private drive to Stoke Park.

The drive is about a mile long and descends to the lush levels of the peaceful valley of the little river Tove. There are found the remarkable remains of the building designed by Inigo Jones for Sir Francis Crane, who founded the Mortlake Tapestry Factory, and erected in 1629-35. It was the first English country house to show the typical Palladian plan of a central block with balancing pavilions. The central block was burned down in 1886 and its unfortunate replacement removed after 1954, when the owner began the enormous task of reviving the dilapidated remains.

Both pavilions have been made good, along with the colonnade and the gardens rescued from their former state of wilderness. In earlier times the west pavilion had been a library and was later converted into a ballroom while the east pavilion was a chapel. Now the latter has been converted into a dwelling but the ballroom remains and the gardens are as peaceful a place as any in the county.

Sulgrave Manor, near Banbury OX17 2SD. Telephone: Sulgrave (029 576) 205. Off the B4525 Northampton-Banbury road 7 miles (11

(Left) *Stoke Park Pavilions, Stoke Bruerne.*
(Right) *Triangular Lodge, Rushton.*

km) east of Banbury.

Until the Dissolution in 1539 the manor of Sulgrave belonged to the priory of St Andrew at Northampton. In that year it was sold to Laurence Washington, who built the present house and whose descendants lived there for the next 120 years. So it was the birthplace of the Reverend Lawrence Washington, whose son, Colonel John Washington, left England in 1656 to take up land in Virginia later known as Mount Vernon. A reminder of this is the family coat of arms carved in a spandrel of the main doorway. The three mullets and two bars are said to have inspired the 'stars and stripes' of the American flag. The family connection with George Washington, the first President of the United States of America, caused the gift of the manor house by a body of British subscribers in 1914 to the peoples of both countries to celebrate one hundred years of peace between them. The National Society of the Colonial Dames of America has endowed the house and helps with its upkeep.

There are many portraits of 'the father of his country' inside and quantities of period furniture. A full set of cooking and domestic implements of eighteenth-century date is ranged in the Great Kitchen. There are pleasant gardens.

Triangular Lodge, Rushton NN14 1RP. Telephone: Kettering (0536) 710761. English Heritage. Off the A6 2 miles (3 km) east of Desborough on the minor road to Rushton.

Sir Thomas Tresham has left his very individual mark on the county landscape in several places but this is his most extraordinary creation. The Warrener's Lodge, as it was sometimes known, was built in 1593-5 after he had spent thirteen years in prison as a 'Popish recusant' and is a profession of his faith and triune beliefs in stone. Everything about it is in threes. The Triangular Lodge must be one of the strangest small buildings ever devised.

Wakefield Lodge, Potterspury, Towcester NN12 7QX. Telephone: Paulerspury (032 733) 212. 5 miles (8 km) south-east of Towcester off the A5. Open by appointment only.

Although the Dukes of Grafton left the county soon after the First World War there are many reminders of the long presence of the Fitzroy family (the first Duke was the natural son of Charles II), including the great house known as Wakefield Lodge. It was built about 1745 by William Kent for the second Duke, who was Chief Ranger of Whittlewood Forest. Kent was close in spirit to Vanbrugh and the Lodge appears massive.

6
Museums and art galleries

Dates and times of opening are liable to vary and some of the smaller museums have very restricted opening times. Intending visitors should always find out the opening hours and dates before making a special journey.

ASHTON
Ashton Mill Fish and Bygones Museum, Ashton Wold, Peterborough PE8 5LZ. Telephone: Oundle (0832) 72264. The Ashton Wold estate is 2 miles (3 km) east of the A605 at Oundle.

Here is an exhibition of fish and objects related to angling in the past. Ways of promoting clean water are illustrated as well as other aspects of conservation, including water-pumping machinery. A traditional black-smith's forge and tools can also be seen.

EARLS BARTON
Earls Barton Museum of Local Life, Earls Barton, Northampton. Telephone: Northampton (0604) 810349.

The museum, at the rear of the Baptist church, contains bygones, work tools, old photographs and documents illustrating the life of local people when it was very different from that of today.

EAST CARLTON
East Carlton Industrial Heritage Centre, East Carlton Countryside Park, East Carlton, Market Harborough LE16 8YD. Telephone: Rockingham (0536) 770977.

The former coach-house at the hall at East Carlton Countryside Park (chapter 2) contains a record of the iron and steel industry in the Corby area. The display begins by showing the geology and early history of ironworking and goes on to show its development in the nineteenth and twentieth centuries, illustrated by models, drawings, photographs and video films. Processes from quarrying to steelmaking and tube forming are explained.

The growth of Corby is recorded (chapter 10) and visitors can find themselves at a control panel of a blast-furnace or standing inside a dragline bucket big enough to hold a rugby team.

KETTERING
Alfred East Art Gallery, Sheep Street, Kettering NN16 0AN. Telephone: Kettering (0536) 85211.

Sir Alfred East RA was born at Kettering and gave a number of his paintings to the town just before his death in 1913. They were housed in a gallery built by the local council on the south side of the library and have been added to since by purchase and gift. The permanent collection now consists of oils, watercolours, etchings and prints, and loan exhibitions are also held.

NASEBY
Naseby Battle and Farm Museum, Purlieu Farm, Naseby, Northampton NN6 7DD. Telephone: Northampton (0604) 740241.

A notable piece of private enterprise by a retired farmer, the museum is off the B4036 road from Daventry to Market Harborough.

On display is a sizable miniature layout of the battlefield with a taped commentary and items to do with it, such as swords, helmets and armour, a flintlock, muskets and cannon-balls. Also there are household and farm bygones reminding one of the days when such things as stock pots, butter pats and the wooden pegs bought from gypsies were in common use. The old farm machinery includes a collection of vintage tractors.

NORTHAMPTON
Abington Museum and Museum of the Northamptonshire Regiment, Abington Park, Northampton. Telephone: Northampton (0604) 31454.

The former manor house was once occupied by the Bernards and later by the Thursbys. Shakespeare's favourite granddaughter married into the first family and a mulberry tree was planted by David Garrick 'at the request of Ann Thursby, as a growing testimony to their friendship'.

The building now houses old domestic items, toys, antique furniture and ancient firefighting equipment. It is also the home of the museum of the county regiment, the 'Steelbacks', and gives a pictorial exhibition of the regimental history from 1741 to 1960, when it was absorbed into the composite Anglian Regiment. There is also a display in connection with the Northamptonshire Yeomanry, a cavalry unit which became an armoured regiment in the Second World War.

The former manor house and the adjacent church are in a pleasant public park. Because emparking took place at an early date, ridge and furrow, the relics of medieval ploughing in the open fields, can still be traced under the grass in places and remains of the medieval village have been found.

Billing Museum of Milling, Little Billing, Northampton. Telephone: Northampton (0604) 40818.

Billing Mill is in the precincts of Billing Aquadrome (chapter 8) off the A45 3 miles

33

(5 km) east of Northampton. It is a watermill restored to working condition and houses a fine collection of artefacts used in the trade. When the machinery is set in motion and the water from the race rushes to turn the great wheel the effect is stunning.

Hunsbury Hill Industrial Museum, Hunsbury Hill Road, Danes Camp Way, Northampton. Telephone: Northampton (0604) 499550.

Hunsbury Hill has had a long and varied history (see chapters 3 and 7) and on this site of former ironstone workings (1873-1921) there is a collection of steam and diesel railway engines and of artefacts connected with the now defunct ironstone industry in the county. A track 2 miles (3 km) in length has been laid, partly on the original track bed, and passenger services are run on Sundays and bank holidays in summer. In 1984 the main engine shed and museum buildings were erected and house the display, the locomotives and repair equipment.

Museum of Leathercraft, 60 Bridge Street, Northampton NN1 1PA. Telephone: Northampton (0604) 34881 extension 382.

This museum complements the footwear collection at the Central Museum. It shows the many and varied uses of leather from prehistoric times to the present. Among the many exhibits is a leather wallet inscribed 'Saml Pepys Esq'. The premises are those of the former Bluecoat Corporation Charity School

The Waterways Museum, Stoke Bruerne.

built in 1811, with statues of 'Bluecoat boys' in niches at the front of the building.

Northampton Central Museum and Art Gallery, Guildhall Road, Northampton NN1 1DP. Telephone: Northampton (0604) 34881 extension 391.

There is a well presented display tracing the history of the town from its earliest days, starting with a neolithic causewayed camp found on Briar Hill when the Southern Development of the borough was begun. Likewise some of the information and relics concerned with the medieval town came to light from excavations conducted for the Development Corporation following demolition of old properties near St Peter's church. There is what is believed to be the most comprehensive footwear collection anywhere and a recreation of a hand shoemaker's workshop. In addition to the permanent displays frequent exhibitions of material from the stores take place.

Royal Pioneer Corps Museum, Simpson Barracks, Wootton, Northampton NN4 0HX. Telephone: Northampton (0604) 762742 extension 34. Beside the B526 2 miles (3 km) south-east of the town centre.

The barracks are the national headquarters of the Corps and the museum has items of military interest relating to its history.

PAULERSPURY
The Sir Henry Royce Memorial Foundation, The Hunt House, Paulerspury. Telephone: Paulerspury (032 733) 797. Paulerspury is on the west side of the A5 3 miles (5 km) south of Towcester.

The Hunt House formerly belonged to the Grafton Hunt. In it is a comprehensive collection of documents, photographs and memorabilia illustrating the history of the premier marque in British motoring, the Rolls-Royce, and the life of its principal creator, the engineering genius Sir Henry Royce.

RUSHDEN
Rushden Railway Station Museum, Station Approach, Rushden NN10 0RH. Telephone: Rushden (0933) 318988.

The railway station is now a museum run by the Rushden Historical Transport Society. The Victorian-style buffet is open each evening, with gas lighting and enamel signs. There is an annual rally of historic transport. The society hopes to relay the track along the old line to Higham Ferrers.

STOKE BRUERNE
Rural Life and Farm Museum, Stoke Bruerne, Towcester NN12 7SE. Telephone: Roade (0604) 863839.

Wellingborough Heritage Centre.

Housed in a former Wesleyan chapel built by local farmworkers, the museum has sections embracing a farm kitchen, a dairy, a scullery, blacksmith's and woodworking tools and farm implements.

The Waterways Museum, Stoke Bruerne, Towcester NN12 7SE. Telephone: Roade (0604) 862229.

It would be difficult to find a more suitable place for a canal museum. The Grand Junction Canal (now the Grand Union) was a trunk route in the heyday of canals, joining the Oxford Canal at Braunston to the Thames at Brentford when it opened in 1800. A short walk along the towing path in a northerly direction brings one to the mouth of the 1¾ miles (2.8 km) Blisworth Tunnel, an engineering wonder when it was opened in 1805 (chapter 10). To the south, a flight of five locks leads down to the valley of the river Tove, which flows through the canal about a mile further on.

Standing at the head of the locks, behind a typical bowed bridge, the museum is located in a former three-storey grain warehouse and facing it across the water is the Boat Inn, with a decorated narrowboat beside it. Within the museum are exhibits showing every aspect of canal life during its history of two hundred years. A full-size replica of a butty boat — the second boat towed behind — shows how life was lived in such a confined space and there are belts and bonnets, tools, tokens, Measham ware teapots and the traditional painted ware, much of which was produced at Braunston (chapter 7).

WELLINGBOROUGH

Wellingborough Heritage Centre, Croyland Hall, Burystead Place, Wellingborough. Telephone: Wellingborough (0933) 76838.

This museum was opened in 1987 by the town's Civic Society in Croyland Hall, near the Tithe Barn (chapter 10) and the Sharman Road car park, off Oxford Street. The name of the hall derives from the historical connection with Crowland Abbey, dating from AD 948, when the land was given to the abbey; abbots were lords of the manor until the Dissolution. The centre is on the ground floor. It has a growing collection of documents, photographs and artefacts relating to the locality. Special exhibitions occur periodically and craft demonstrations such as lacemaking are designed to make the centre a living entity and not just a museum. A small section is devoted to one of the great flying heroes of the First World War, Mick Mannock, from Wellingborough, who won the DSO, MC and bar and (posthumously) the Victoria Cross after shooting down 73 enemy aircraft.

WOLLASTON

Wollaston Museum, 104 High Street, Wollaston NN9 7RJ. Telephone: Wellingborough (0933) 664645.

Keen and knowledgeable local historians have set up this commendable enterprise, featuring local archaelogical finds, old prints, photographs and documents concerned with bygone village life. Also there are exhibits to do with lacemaking and footwear manufacture, farming and local artists.

Barnwell Lock on the river Nene.

7
Industrial heritage

Ashton Mill, Ashton Wold, Peterborough PE8 5LZ. (OS 142; TL 051875). Telephone: Oundle (0832) 73575.

There was a mill here at the time of Domesday and the present mill ground corn until 1900, when the first Lord Rothschild had it converted to supply piped water for the village of Ashton and the group of houses at Ashton Wold. Also it was used to supply electricity to the main buildings and farm. If the river was sufficiently high, water worked the turbines, otherwise diesel engines were used. Two turbines and two oil engines have been restored as a reminder of this advanced Victorian engineering. For Ashton Mill Fish and Bygones Museum, see chapter 6.

Barnwell Mill and Lock, near Oundle (OS 141; TL 038870).

The stone-built mill with a wooden lucam dates partly from 1746 and is a good example of a mill associated with river navigation. The lock typifies many on the Nene, with at one end a pair of standard gates and at the other a massive guillotine gate to prevent flooding.

Braunston Canal Basin, Braunston, near Rugby (OS 152; SP 540659).

The basin is at the former junction of the Grand Union Canal and the Oxford Canal, the latter having been diverted to a short distance away. From here the Grand Junction Canal, as it was originally named, was cut to join the Thames at Brentford. The basin has gained fresh vitality from the growth of pleasure cruising and since the 1950s a marina has been privately developed, linking two old reservoirs with the canal itself.

Narrowboats were once built here for commercial use and decorated in the traditional fashion long before it was considered an art form. Frank Nurser, who inherited the boatyard in its last decades of commercial activity and who died in 1952, carried on the craft in what was a recognisable Braunston manner and influenced others in their geometrical designs and depictions of roses and castles.

Charwelton Packhorse Bridge, Charwelton, near Daventry (OS 152; SP 536562).

Only 3 feet (0.9 metre) wide, with two pointed arches, the bridge is squeezed by the A361 road, which has been widened against it. It is said to be the only unaltered and truly medieval bridge in the county.

Cosgrove, near Milton Keynes (OS 152; SP 800418).

Follow the signs to Cosgrove Lodge Park a mile (1.5 km) east of the A508 and there is the 'stupendous' embankment (as it was justly described when the canal was opened in 1805) carrying the waterway across the Ouse valley and into Buckinghamshire. The canal is carried over the river by a cast iron aqueduct known as the Iron Trunk, made at the Ketley Iron Works and installed in 1811 after a three-arch brick construction collapsed.

Cosgrove village has another unusual canal feature. The canal was driven straight through the village so that to get directly from one end of the main street to the other you have to go through a small pedestrian tunnel.

Finedon Water Tower, Finedon (OS 141; SP 926717).

On the A6 road at the eastern end of the town there is an elaborate Victorian structure in polychromatic brick with a castellated top.

Grand Union Canal, Northampton Arm (OS 152; SP 720550 to 753597).

The narrow canal link to Northampton from the main canal at Gayton was opened in 1815 amid great rejoicing. From 1805 the town had been connected with the main 'cut' by a horse-drawn tramway which gave little satisfaction. The 4⅞ mile (7.8 km) branch has seventeen locks, there being a flight of eleven at Rothersthorpe, with a lock-keeper's cottage and three timber lifting bridges between SP 723560 and 727571.

Harringworth Viaduct (OS 141; SP 913970). 2 miles (3 km) east of Uppingham on the A47, turn south along a minor road for 3 miles (5 km).

This viaduct was built by the Midland Railway across the Welland valley in 1877-9. ¾ mile (1.2 km) in length with 82 arches, it is an impressive spectacle.

Helmdon Viaduct (OS 152; SP 583437). On a minor road 5 miles (8 km) north of Brackley.

A nine-arch viaduct across the infant river Tove is a reminder of the scale of the engineering on the Great Central Railway into London Marylebone, Britain's last main line, built in the late 1890s and closed in 1966. In Northamptonshire it has left a gigantic scar on the landscape but a section from Loughborough to Rothley in Leicestershire has been preserved by enthusiasts. The viaduct also spanned the old Stratford-on-Avon and Midland Junction line from Towcester to Banbury, so that until 1951, when passenger services ceased on that line, Helmdon had two railway stations and people could travel north, south, east or west by train.

Irchester Country Park (OS 152; SP 913658). See also chapter 2.

Here are to be found some of the most important remains of the iron ore industry. It is possible to trace the course of narrow-gauge tramway routes (1863-1906) and the later standard-gauge ironstone railway tracks used by the South Durham Steel and Iron company until 1969. The Wembley Pit was so named after the exhibition of 1924 and in 1938 left a deep gulley, in addition to the 'hill and dale' formation of the backfill in the worked-out portion of the quarry, while there can be seen also the remains of the calcine clamps which were an important feature of local iron ore extraction.

The Irchester Narrow Gauge Railway Trust has its shed, museum and narrow-gauge locomotives in the park and operates steam-hauled trains along the original tramway route. Its steam locomotive, once used in the Wellingborough quarries, is the most outstanding example of locomotive restoration in Northamptonshire.

Kettering

The Midland Railway opened the Leicester to Hitchin line in 1857 and Kettering station retains the island platform awnings and decorative ironwork from that date. The main building with its terracotta ornamentation belongs to the rebuilding in about 1890.

In Lower Street in the centre of Kettering are some maltings, a fine Victorian brick building. Also there are a number of shoe factories and other buildings illustrating Ket-

Water tower, Finedon.

37

tering's industrial growth (chapter 10), in Green Lane, Newman Street and Victoria Street. In Scotland Street is the factory of Wicksteed Leisure, founded in the 1870s by Charles Wicksteed as a small engineering firm. He created Wicksteed Park (chapter 8). The firm now specialises in fairground and other leisure equipment.

Kilsby Tunnel (south entrance: OS 152; SP 578698; north entrance: OS 152; SP 565713).

The building of the London to Birmingham railway (opened 1838), the first trunk line into London, belongs to the heroic age of British engineering. The youthful engineer in charge, Robert Stephenson, son of George, was grappling with new problems and none more so than with the Kilsby Tunnel. Frequent flooding, only overcome by the constant use of powerful steam pumps, held up the work so that for a time the middle section of the journey was by road, from Bletchley to Rugby. The tunnel is 1 mile 682 yards (2232 metres) long. The north entrance can be seen from the A5 road north of Kilsby village and the southern one from the lane between the A5 and Ashby St Ledgers. The tunnel has huge ventilation shafts of 60 feet (18 metres) diameter with crenellated tops. One of these stands north of the A5 about half a mile (800 metres) east of Kilsby (OS 140; SP 569708).

Nether Heyford (OS 152; SP 654580).

On a minor road leading into Nether Heyford from the A5, Furnace Lane is a name that serves as a reminder of the former existence of three blast-furnaces opened in 1857 and closed in 1891. Their remains are to be found between the canal and the railway and the entrance house is still *in situ.*

Northampton Boot and Shoe Trail.

Northampton Library and Leisure Services have published a trail which leads past 28 premises having past or present connections with the former staple trade of the town, centred on the St Michael's Road area. Unfortunately the first and last of the buildings have both been demolished, the former so that the site can be redeveloped, the latter because of road widening.

North of the town centre, along the Kingsthorpe Road, is the highly ornate structure of Barrett's Footshape Works. Built in 1913, it was so called after the mail order sales system of using an outline of one's own foot to ensure a fit.

Northamptonshire Ironstone Railway Trust, Hunsbury Hill. (See also chapter 6.)

The growth of the machine age following the industrial revolution caused a great increase in demand for iron and from the mid nineteenth

Helmdon viaduct, on the old Great Central line.

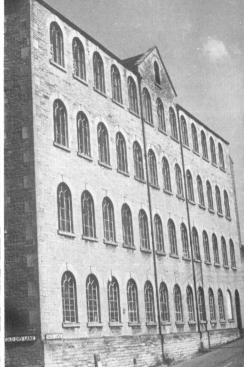

(Left) *The railway station, Kettering.*
(Right) *Wallis' Mill, Brigstock.*

century many large-scale ironstone quarries and associated iron-smelting furnaces were opened in the county. (Only Corby has had steelmaking facilities.)

The Camp Pit, as it was called when quarrying began in 1873 because of the iron age fort known as Danes' Camp, supplied ore for furnaces located half a mile (800 metres) away near the Northampton arm of the canal and the Blisworth to Peterborough railway. Both were used to bring ore from other quarries and carry away slag and pig-iron. The wagons from the Camp Pit carried the ore by gravity down the hill and when empty were hauled back by horses retired from the drays of Phipps' Brewery Company. In 1912 the horses were replaced by three locomotives, the only mechanisation ever used in this quarry.

Ravensthorpe Reservoir (OS 141; SP 682704). North of Northampton on the A50, at Spratton, turn west on a minor road for 2 miles (3 km).

The reservoir was made in 1890 to supply water to Northampton. In July 1987 Anglia Water opened the pump-house after modernisation. The project was praised for preserving good Victorian architecture while adapting its use to modern needs. With Hollowell Reservoir, it now supplies water to Long Buckby and other villages in the area, with any surplus going to the county town.

Staverton Toll-house, Staverton, near Daventry (OS 152; SP 547614).

This toll-house of the Northampton and Warwick Turnpike Trust is on the A425 3 miles (5 km) south-west of Daventry.

Stoke Bruerne, Waterways Museum and Blisworth Tunnel (see chapter 6).

Victoria Mill, Wellingborough (OS 152; SP 902665).

Built by J. B. Whitworth in 1886 as a four-storey steam-powered roller mill, it stands beside the Nene with road, rail and canal access. Grain was brought by water until 1969. The mill was electrified in 1958 and still works.

Wallis' Mill, Brigstock, near Corby (OS 141; TL 945856).

In 1873 the building was opened as a clothing factory with extensive windows to give light working conditions for machinists. In 1984, when converted into offices for an architectural practice, the imposing four-storey Weldon stone building won an award for sympathetic re-use of industrial premises.

39

8
Other places to visit

Billing Aquadrome, Northampton NN3 4DA. Telephone: Northampton (0604) 408181. South of the A45, 3 miles (5 km) east of Northampton.

Like many other pleasure centres in the county the Aquadrome is based on old gravel workings but it must be one of the oldest, since it began in the 1930s. In its 270 acres (110 ha) of parkland, woods and lakes it provides camping and caravan sites, boating, coarse fishing, wind surfing and sailing facilities. There are children's playgrounds, a miniature railway, an amusement centre with funfair, a giant Astroglide and picnic areas with restaurants and bars.

Cosgrove Lodge Park Leisure Centre, Milton Keynes. Telephone: Milton Keynes (0908) 563360. Off the A508 2 miles (3 km) north of Old Stratford.

The river Ouse here forms the county boundary with Buckinghamshire so the gravel pits dug at the time of the building of the M1 lie across it. Seven lagoons in 110 acres (45 ha) of parkland provide similar facilities to those at Billing and one 25 acre (10 ha) pool is set aside for water skiing. The Grand Union Canal embankment adjoins (chapter 7).

Coton Manor Gardens, near Ravensthorpe, Northampton. Telephone: Northampton (0604) 740219.

Coton Manor lies between the A50 and A428 roads, near Ravensthorpe Reservoir (chapter 7). It stands on high ground overlooking the reservoir, with views over 'shire country'. The combination of specialist horticulture, including a delightful water garden, and an assembly of wading birds including flamingoes make Coton a popular place to visit.

Delapre Golf Complex, Eagle Drive, Nene Valley Way, Northampton NN4 0DU. Telephone: Northampton (0604) 764036. To reach this, leave the dual carriageway halfway between the Eleanor Cross roundabout and the one giving access to the Bedford Road.

The complex is claimed to be the finest public one of its kind in Europe, with every aspect of golf catered for, and used by 200,000 players every year. Teaching facilities comprise 25 covered floodlit practice bays, pitch and putt, putting greens, grass practice areas with bunkers and sloping lies and an eighteen-hole main course.

Edgcote battlefield, 26th July 1469 (OS 151; SP 519468).

Edward IV had become king but had quar-relled with Warwick the 'Kingmaker' because of his marriage to Elizabeth Woodville (chapter 9).

In June 1469 Edward led his army north to quell a revolt led by Sir John Conyers (Robin of Redesdale), when he heard that Warwick had returned from France and mustered an army. To prevent Warwick and Conyers joining, a strong force of Welsh pikemen under Lords Devon and Pembroke advanced from the west towards Northampton. At Banbury they quarrelled and only Pembroke moved on, camping at Edgcote. Next morning he found Conyers's men facing him in three divisions. Instead of withdrawing to link with Devon, Pembroke with foolhardy bravery attacked, taking his enemies' central position at Danesmoor and advancing towards Culworth Hill, but he was driven back by Conyers's bowmen. He then turned to assault the third group on Edgcote Hill but at the critical moment his men were assailed by a fresh arrival on their right flank. This was the advance guard of Warwick's force led by John Clapham of Skipton and strengthened by mercenaries recruited at Northampton. This turned the battle and the Welshmen who escaped fled towards home along the lane still known as the Welsh Road. The Earl of Pembroke and his son were captured and summarily executed at Northampton.

This site has changed very little and can be viewed by taking the A361 from Banbury to Wardington, turning right and driving round Danesmoor. Edgcote Lodge stands on the hill overlooking Pembroke's position.

Grange Lodge Mini Farm Park, Naseby Road, Welford NN6 7HZ. Telephone: Welford (085 881) 625. The park is signposted on the A50 and is reached a short distance along the Naseby Road.

There are 7 acres (3 ha) of small paddocks and pens where farm animals are to be seen in natural surroundings. Families are invited to meet the animals at close quarters and in this way children can become acquainted with a Shetland pony, Dexter cows and calves and many other creatures and their young in season. Children can also enjoy a well equipped playground and interested adults can study organically grown plants and vegetables.

Guilsborough Grange Wild Life Park, West Haddon Road, Guilsborough, Northampton. Telephone: Northampton (0604) 740278.

Guilsborough Grange is in the same tract of rolling country as Coton and Holdenby and so enjoys similar panoramic views. Its 30 acres

(12 ha) of parkland contain many species of big cats, owls, deer and a great assortment of other birds and mammals. Weather permitting, falconry displays take place daily and there is a tearoom, pet shop and gift shop.

Knuston Hall, Irchester, Wellingborough, NN9 7EU. Telephone: Rushden (0933) 312104.

Knuston Hall is beside the B569 on the outskirts of Rushden, the town where the novelist H. E. Bates grew up, and the elegant building and its commanding situation are reminiscent of the mansion at Spella Ho and other similar places figuring in his earlier novels and stories. Adult education courses have been held here since 1951. Residential sessions, usually of two or three days duration, offer a comprehensive range of subjects and one-day seminars are also held.

Lilford Park, near Oundle, Peterborough PE8 5SG. Telephone: Clopton (080 15) 648 or 665. To the west of the A605 halfway between Oundle and Thrapston.

Lilford Hall is a listed Jacobean building set in 240 acres (97 ha) of grass and woodland. From 1711 it has been owned by the Powys family, the head of which became Lord Lilford in 1797. In the years 1860-90 the then Lord Lilford created the world-famous Lilford aviaries and was president of the British Ornithologists' Union for thirty years until his death. The present Lord Lilford has restored the aviaries and flamingo pool and there is a large selection of native and exotic birds, including one of the biggest collections of owls in England. (It was the fourth Lord Lilford who was mainly responsible for introducing the little owl into Britain in the 1890s.)

Other attractive features include a children's farm where favourite animals can be safely enjoyed, an adventure playground with a tree house, extensive rock gardens, a pinetum including picnic sites, a model car racing track, craft workshops, a puppet theatre and a great deal more. One can drive one's car at large and it is not confined to a car park.

Naseby battlefield, 14th June 1645 (OS 141; SP 682801).

By the time Charles I left Daventry (chapter 9) the Parliamentary forces under Fairfax had advanced to Kislingbury, about 4 miles (6 km) west of Northampton, and their scouts at Flore saw the smoke from the burning huts vacated on Borough Hill. When Cromwell appeared with a reinforcement of six hundred horse it was decided to bring the Royalists to battle. Prince Rupert, now commander-in-chief, took position on Dust Hill, north of Naseby, and the numerically superior New Model Army found a facing ridge where now stands

Battle monument, Naseby.

the monument on the road from Naseby to Sibbertoft. Rupert's initial charge on the opposing left wing, followed by that of the Earl of Northampton, swept most of Ireton's force away but the uncontrolled pursuit left the field to Cromwell on the other flank. He defeated the opposing cavalry and wheeled to destroy the Royalist centre, all of whom were killed, wounded or captured. The five thousand prisoners were marched to Northampton and many were imprisoned in the churches.

The King's cause never recovered from this blow. An obelisk on the B4036 near Naseby village, erected by the lord of the manor in 1823, has an inscription saying that the battle led to the subversion of the throne and gave 'a useful lesson to British kings never to exceed the bounds of their prerogative'.

When Naseby Field was enclosed following the award of 1822 many relics of the fight were unearthed. Take away most of the hedges and it is possible to imagine the Cavaliers charging recklessly and the Ironsides manoeuvring purposefully to win the day. See chapter 6 for the Naseby Battle and Farm Museum.

Northampton battlefield, 10th July 1460 (OS 152; SP 759597).

Having spent the previous night camped on Hunsbury Hill, Edward, Earl of March (later

41

Edward IV), and the Earl of Warwick descended with their Yorkist force towards the town where the Lancastrian troops were entrenched in the water-meadows near Delapre Abbey, with their backs to the river. When battle was joined Lord Grey of Ruthin, a cousin of the Queen and Commander of the right flank, switched sides and a rout followed: 'Many were slain, and many were fled, and were drowned in the river.' The Duke of Buckingham and the Earl of Shrewsbury were among the notables who perished, 'slain by the Kentishmen'. The captured Henry VI was taken to London and the Duke of York came from Ireland to claim the throne. The scene of the battle has been cut up by railway lines and industrial sites so that it is difficult to envisage it as it was.

Overstone Solarium, Ecton Lane, Sywell, Northampton NN6 0BD. Telephone: Northampton (0604) 45255. Overstone Park lies between the A43 Kettering road and the A4500 Wellingborough road, 4 miles (6.5 km) from the town centre.

Long before the term 'leisure park' was devised Overstone was a magnet for Northampton folk. The central building was constructed in the 1930s, about the same time that Horton Hall was demolished, and relics of that mansion are to be found in the marble fireplace in the ballroom and the oak one in the Oak Room. Around the house is parkland with woods, lakes and picnic areas. There is a swimming pool, boating, fishing, putting and crazy golf, squash, tennis and a caravan site. On Sundays and bank holidays in summer the 60 cm (2 foot) gauge light railway, powered by a 1946 motor rail diesel locomotive, runs over a track nearly a mile (1.5 km) in length.

Skew Bridge Country Club and Ski School, Rushden. Telephone: Rushden (0933) 311809 (club house) or 59939 (ski school). The club is on the western fringe of Rushden, close to the junction of the A6 and the A45.

Named after the railway bridge near its entrance, the club began in 1956 with a 23 acre (9 ha) lake and a Nissen hut for a clubhouse but has expanded greatly, with a new clubhouse and squash courts, moorings in the lake with two more lakes made suitable for water skiing, a hotel, an outdoor swimming pool, all-weather tennis courts and facilities for cricket, clay-pigeon shooting and other sports. Non-members have access to the ski school based on a dry slope 300 feet (90 metres) long.

Turner's Musical Merry-go-round, Newport Pagnell Road, Wootton, Northampton NN4 0HU. Telephone: Northampton (0604) 63314. Beside the B526 2 miles (3 km) south of the town centre.

This entertainment centre embodies a most original concept and has become deservedly popular. Many come to enjoy the carousel, Wurlitzer organ and other attractive features and to participate in the tea and supper dances, concerts, parties and much else in the custom-built hall.

Wicksteed Leisure Park, London Road, Kettering. Telephone: Kettering (0536) 512475. The park is in the Ise valley on the A6 road from Kettering to Burton Latimer.

While most funfairs must make a profit to survive, Wicksteed Park has philanthropic origins. Charles Wicksteed was the son of a Leeds Unitarian minister and in 1876 at the age of 24 he set up a small factory to make steam ploughing equipment and other metal items. He was a red-hot radical by inclination and as his prosperity increased he began to create a pleasure ground for children, which opened in 1920. Today there are 2 acres (0.8 ha) of free playground with fifty items on it, many of which are original designs of the founder. Further afield there are many paid-for features, including a miniature railway, skateboard track, boating, swimming and paddling pools, and additions are constantly being made to make a place where enjoyment for children could scarcely be bettered.

9
Folklore, famous people and events

Northamptonshire may appear to be a less romantic county than many but it has a crop of myths and legends comparable to any from the Celtic west. It has even been suggested that St Patrick was a native of the Roman town of *Bannaventa* near Daventry who was abducted by raiders and removed to Ireland.

Other less famous saints have county connections. In the dark ages the area we know as Northamptonshire was part of Mercia and Penda, the last pagan king, is believed to have had a royal household at **King's Sutton**. His grandson, St Rumbold (or Rumwold), was born of Christian parents and, although he lived only three days, miraculously and eloquently preached Christianity, leaving such a memory that springs feeding wells were named after him at Brackley and King's Sutton. The latter is in a field near the railway station and is still considered a source of good drinking water.

During the seventeenth century a chalybeate spring was discovered in **Astrop Park**, east of King's Sutton, and developed into a spa by doctors from Oxford, who said it had medicinal properties and called it after St Rumbold. A replica of the old well-head is found along the Charlton Road.

A pamphlet of 1668 by a 'learned physician' claimed that the water 'penetrates through every occult passage where other medecines cannot come', which seems to pre-date a modern television advertisement by three hundred years. By the mid eighteenth century it was said of Astrop that 'Nature and Art have contributed to make it a paradise of pleasure'. As late as 1813 Rowlandson was drawing a busy scene at 'Aystrop Wells' but today only parkland can be seen where once stood the pleasure rooms of a popular spa.

As odd as the story of St Rumbold is that of St Werburga, extolled by Drayton when writing of **Weedon Bec:**

'Saint Werburge, princely born, a most
    religious maid,
From these peculiar fields, by prayer, the
    wild geese drave.'

This refers to the legend that the daughter of Wulfhere, another Mercian king, got rid of a plague of geese after founding a Christian cell in the village. An extra gloss suggests that she brought back to life a goose which had been killed and cooked so that it could join its fellows on their departure.

A later saint was Ragener, nephew of King Edmund, who was killed by the Danes in AD 870. It is claimed that during the reign of Edward the Confessor his tomb was discovered in St Peter's church, **Northampton,** and

a late fifteenth-century will suggests that his shrine was still preserved there at that time.

An earlier but less shadowy figure in ecclesiastical history was St Wilfrid, Abbot of Ripon and Bishop of York, who was said by the Venerable Bede to have founded a monastery at **Oundle** and to have died there in 709.

Most extensive tracts of woodland harbour the myth of a ghostly hunter and in **Whittlewood** a spectral 'wild rider' was believed to chase for ever a female wraith, along with his pack of 'hell hounds'.

Another legend is based on the name of **Stowe-Nine-Churches.** The factual reason for this seems to be that the lord of the manor had the right of presentation of the clergy to nine churches, but the legend is more interesting. Eight times the men of Stowe tried to build a church at the foot of the hill on which the village stands (chapter 4) and each time their work was destroyed by night, until one intrepid peasant volunteered to keep watch. In the dark of a moonless night he could only see that the destroyer was a 'crettur no bigger nor a hog' but its superhuman strength soon demolished the fabric of the previous day. This caused the builders to shift their efforts to the hilltop, where the Saxon tower of Church Stowe now stands.

One of the two manors at **Titchmarsh,** near Thrapston, was held by the Lovell family from 1286 until 1485. Sir John Lovell in 1359 obtained a charter for a weekly market on Monday and an annual eight-day fair to begin on the eve of Holy Trinity and some have attributed to him the building of the church tower, claimed to be the finest parish church tower in England outside Somerset.

Northamptonshire has much genuine history with legendary undertones. Edward IV was one of many monarchs to hunt in Whittlewood and in 1464 he met and married Elizabeth Woodville, a member of the family seated at Grafton — later Grafton Regis. Traditionally their first meeting took place at the **Queens Oak,** which still stands near Potterspury Lodge and adjacent to the Grafton Way (chapter 2). Later a sequence of tragedies overtook Queen Elizabeth, including the deaths of her father, Earl Rivers, two of her brothers and three of her sons, including the pathetic pair of princes who entered the Tower of London and were seen no more.

Like the Woodvilles, the Catesbys of **Ashby St Ledgers** had a tragic role in English history. Robert Catesby was the leader of the Gunpowder Plot and traditionally the conspirators met in the timbered gatehouse of his manor. The bold Catesby died fighting but the other

Northamptonshire plotter perished miserably in the Tower. This was Francis Tresham of **Rushton**, son of Thomas, builder of the Triangular Lodge (chapter 5). Francis reputedly sent the warning letter to his brother-in-law Lord Monteagle and so exposed the plot.

The fate of Mary, Queen of Scots, was mentioned in chapter 3. It is said that her ghost has been seen at the Talbot Inn at **Oundle**, where there is a fine staircase thought to have come from Fotheringhay, although close inspection shows no sign of a move.

In 1607 at **Newton in the Willows** (chapter 3) took place a one-sided affray when about a thousand of the local peasantry revolted against the enclosures of the Tresham family and threw down the hedges. Lord Montagu of Boughton and Sir Anthony Mildmay of Apethorpe brought forces and brutally snuffed out the resistance. The leader of the levellers was John Reynolds, who called himself Captain Pouch because of his great leather pouch, in which he told his followers 'there was sufficient matter to defend them against all comers', but when opened after his capture it was found to contain only a piece of green cheese.

At about the same time another harsh landlord was incurring such odium that he allegedly haunted his village long afterwards. This was Sir Robert Banastre of **Passenham** (chapter 4). According to a Victorian account, he was so frequent a revenant that 'six men, eminent for piety, were required to lay his spirit . . . in the bottom of the mill dam'. This notion was embodied in a short story, 'Soft Voices at Passenham', written by T. H. White, who was once a master at Stowe School, a few miles away.

Another and better documented haunting took place at the Wheatsheaf Inn at **Daventry.** Charles I arrived there with his army on 7th June 1645 and stayed six nights. According to 'a person of Newarke att that time in his Majesties' Horse', the ghost of his former counsellor, Strafford, appeared on two successive nights and warned him not to stay in the vicinity, causing the king great agitation. Unfortunately for him, he was slow to respond and by the time he decided to move the Parliamentary army under Fairfax had come so close that the disastrous defeat at Naseby was inevitable.

The depredations of the **Culworth** Gang in the late eighteenth century also gave rise to legends. The village now quieter than most but the Banbury Lane and the Welsh Road cross there and along these operated a band of highwaymen and burglars for more than a decade before 1787, spreading terror not only in their own county but in neighbouring Buckinghamshire, Oxfordshire and Warwickshire. In that year they were rounded up and

the four principal malefactors were hanged on 3rd August on Northampton Heath (now the racecourse) before a crowd of five thousand.

A place for regular skulduggery was the famous **Boughton Green** Fair, held about 4 miles (6 km) north of Northampton town centre on a green triangle of about 17 acres (7 ha) near the old ruined church of St John the Baptist. It certainly took place from 1351, when it was legally established by charter, until 1916, on 24th, 25th and 26th June. By about 1870 the first day was devoted to the sale of 'implements of husbandry, wooden ware etc', the second 'principally to pleasure' and on the third a large horse and cattle fair was held. 'Many rural sports and games, as racing, wrestling and the single stick exercise' were once practised there. It also attracted undesirables. On 21st July 1826 George Catherall, aged 29, alias 'Captain Slash', was hanged at Northampton jail because he led a gang of footpads who violently assaulted and robbed people on the night following the fair, saying to one of his prostrate victims: 'Damn your eyes, blood or money!'

There is more than one link between the county and the early heroes of the United States. George Washington had no interest in his ancestors but when Benjamin Franklin arrived on an official visit in 1757 as representative of the Pennsylvania State Assembly he headed for **Ecton**. This is now the first place on the A4500 outside the bounds of greater Northampton but must have been far removed from the county town in those days. The church registers had entries relating to the Franklin family going back to 1559, when the record began. The great inventor visited the grave of his uncle Thomas, who had been the village blacksmith, as was Benjamin's grandfather before him. Like his famous nephew, Thomas was a self-taught man of many talents. He died in 1702 and his grave and that of his wife, Eleanor, are still to be seen in the churchyard of St Mary Magdalene, where on the north wall of the church there is a bronze tablet to commemorate Franklin's Ecton connection.

For a small village, **Aldwincle** is remarkable in having two churches and it is even more surprising that an important literary figure was born in the rectory of each. At St Peter's in 1608 Thomas Fuller was born. He grew up to be the parson whose muscular prose in his *Worthies of England* often affords a good quotation but who is less well remembered as the author of religious histories and dissertations which caused him to be admitted a doctor of divinity and appointed chaplain to King Charles II.

The other rectory, that of All Saints, was the birthplace of John Dryden (1631-1700), one of two contrasting county poets. (All Saints'

44

All Saints' church, Northampton.

church is now redundant but has been restored as an architectural museum.) Dryden was a scion of the family that were squires of Canons Ashby for almost four hundred years (chapter 5). Poet, dramatist and satirist, he is now best remembered for the satirical portraits in *Absalom and Achitophel.* In his lifetime he enjoyed great success with all branches of his writing and became Poet Laureate and Historiographer Royal in 1670.

By contrast John Clare, the peasant poet (1793-1864), was bred in poverty at Helpston in the Soke of Peterborough and so is reckoned a Northamptonshire poet. After early success with his *Poems*, descriptive of rural life (1820), he suffered failure and disappointment, spending his declining years in the lunatic asylum at **Northampton.** He was seen during lucid periods in the town sitting under the portico of All Saints' church.

Of the county's other native sons, Miss Joan Wake (chapter 5) has declared the greatest probably to have been William Carey DD (1761-1834). Raised in poverty and obscurity at **Pury End,** Paulerspury, and apprenticed to a shoemaker at **Piddington,** he had such a combination of intellect and determination that he became a Baptist minister and the first missionary of that denomination in India. There, from 1801 to 1830 he was Oriental Professor at Fort William College, Calcutta, translating the scriptures into about forty oriental languages and publishing grammars and dictionaries in Bengali, Marathi and other tongues.

May Day celebrations have been maintained in some villages, notably at **Flore.** At **Moulton** the May Day is part of a festival in which the Moulton Morris Men and other dancers participate. There is a May Day carol peculiar to the county with many local variants.

It should not be thought that Northamptonshire is notable only for historical connections. The Second World War airfield at **Silverstone** near Towcester became in the 1950s a first-class motor-racing circuit where the British Grand Prix and other Formula I events are held.

Another old airfield at **Brafield-on-the-Green,** just off the A428 road 5 miles (8 km) east of Northampton, is used for stock car and 'banger' racing. Quieter than these is the 'Soap-box Derby' racing held annually at **Blakesley,** near Towcester. Elaborately constructed unpowered vehicles come from far and wide to race down the sloping village street, reaching speeds of up to 50 miles (80 km) an hour, before crowds of five thousand.

An older tradition is the annual Mobbs Memorial Match between the Barbarians and the East Midlands rugby teams. Lieutenant-Colonel Edgar Mobbs played for Northampton and England before the First World War, raised a 'sportsmen's battalion' and was killed in action in 1917. The contest takes place in March at Franklins Gardens, the well appointed ground of the **Northampton** club at St James' End, the Victorian western extension of the town. The club was started in 1880 by the Reverend Wathen Wigg to occupy the

45

Blakesley 'Soap-box Derby'.

youths of 'Jimmy's End', as the locality is called, and the team is known as the 'Saints'.

With so many church towers, there is a great tradition of bellringing in the county. This is exemplified at **Ecton,** where the church of St Mary Magdalene has a notable ring of bells. This is not surprising, for the Franklin family ran a bell foundry in addition to their smithy on the site now occupied by the Three Horseshoes inn. In the church tower is a mural dated 1756 showing six bellringers with raised arms ready to begin. An inscription records: 'We the under-writen Ring the First Six Bell peal 720 upon 6 Bells of this Parish.' Their

names and heights follow, the latter suggesting that they were shorter than men today, for the tallest is only 5 feet 9½ inches (1.77 metres).

Another activity peculiar to the locality is a game of skittles found in Northamptonshire and which has only spread marginally into neighbouring counties. Three 'cheeses' — quite heavy discs — are hurled in turn at nine skittles standing on a sturdy table partly surrounded by a net in the interests of safety. It is a warming and noisy exercise, especially when a 'stack' is registered — that is, all nine skittles are felled at once.

10
Towns and villages

ASHBY ST LEDGERS

Ashby is an estate village, being the former seat of Lord Wimborne, who employed Lutyens to add to his mansion early in the twentieth century. Much earlier it was the home of the Catesbys (chapter 9). The village is hardly medieval but it does give an impression of a place where time has stood still.

ASHTON (near Oundle)

Ashton is a model village, rebuilt about 1900 for the Honourable Charles Rothschild, second son of the first Lord Rothschild. The manor house and cottages are all in Tudor style but the facilities such as bathrooms were well ahead of their time (chapter 7). Charles Rothschild was a great entomologist and expert on fleas. In 1912 he founded the Society for the Promotion of Nature Reserves, now the Royal Society for Nature Conservation, and his work has been carried on by his daughter, Miss Miriam Rothschild, so that nowadays a new reserve is being created every five days. The name of the village inn is most appropriate for it is called after a butterfly, the Chequered Skipper. It stands beside a very pleasant green used annually for the World 'Conker' Championship.

AYNHO

The former seat of the Cartwright family is known as the 'Apricot Village'. Aynho sits in a favourable position above the Cherwell valley and in medieval times the lord of the manor received part of his rent in apricots. Many of the residents still grow them. Aynho is adjacent to the Oxfordshire border and there is much of the appearance of a Cotswold village: even the council houses are stone-built. A pair of stocks contributes to the faintly feudal atmosphere still lingering but the heavy traffic thundering past disturbs the image. A waterways holiday base is located on the Oxford Canal, which follows the course of the Cherwell in the valley below. See chapter 4 for the church and chapter 5 for Aynhoe Park.

BLAKESLEY

This village is not easy to find because it lies in a web of minor roads west of the Watling Street, just off the Banbury Lane, which can be followed from Fosters Booth, adjacent to Pattishall on the A5. On the way Seawell Grounds Farm, one of the imposing Regency-style farmhouses built for the Duke of Grafton about 1840, is passed. The previous house was the scene of the last robbery perpetrated by the Culworth Gang before their arrest in 1787.

The village has some fine ironstone build-ings, including a school where the addition of a pyramid-shaped extension once caused great controversy, and the Bartholomew Arms, a splendid inn the name of which commemorates the family once resident at Blakesley Hall. Charles Bartholomew, a flamboyant squire, in the early twentieth century connected the hall (now demolished) with Blakesley station by means of a miniature railway, powered from 1909 by an engine built by Bassett-Lowke of Northampton which had the appearance of a steam locomotive but was driven by a 14 horsepower internal combustion engine.

BLISWORTH

Blisworth's canal tunnel is still of prime importance — when it was closed for repairs in the 1980s great difficulties for canal cruisers ensued — but men of the village are no longer employed as 'leggers'. These were men who in the days of horse-drawn boats would lie on their backs on a plank on the boat and brace their feet against the tunnel sides and 'walk' the boat along, while the horse was led over the top of the hill. Blisworth used to be an important railway junction on the main line from Euston but the station and branch lines have been closed. Also vanished are the ironstone workings once common hereabouts and the seven limekilns not far from the north end of the canal tunnel.

The variety of colour in the building stone remarked on by Morton is exemplified here. He spoke of the 'white' and 'red' freestone being found in alternate courses and there are houses here, notably Stoneacres in Stoke Road, with contrasting bands of the two colours, giving an unusual effect. In the church of St John the Baptist is the tomb of Roger Wake (died 1503) and his wife with brasses, he in full armour. From him are descended the Wakes of Courteenhall.

BOUGHTON

A village on the northern fringe of greater Northampton, this is not to be confused with Boughton House near Kettering. Apart from memories of the celebrated Boughton Green Fair, there are other more solid relics of the past near this pleasant place.

A number of follies were built here for the second Earl of Strafford, who lived in a house no longer extant. The most conspicuous is the Hawking Tower (OS 152; SP 749660), along-side the A508. It looks like a small church but is a limestone lodge with a two-storey tower. A mile from Boughton along the road to Moulton is Holly Lodge (OS 152; SP 769658) and across the front drive is a Victorian iron gate made in the shape of twelve different farm implements. Only 200 yards (180 metres) away down a pretty lane starting opposite Holly Lodge and called Spectacle Lane is the Spectacle itself, a mock gateway like Holly Lodge with 'towers' on either side. From hereabouts can be seen, near the Pitsford to Moulton road (OS 152; SP 762667), the mock castellation of Bunkers Hill Farm, with a datestone suggesting it was named after the battle in the American War of Independence. Half a mile (800 metres) south of Boughton church, surrounded now by houses, is one more Strafford structure — the Obelisk (OS 152; SP 755653), built in 1764 in memory of the fourth Duke of Devonshire.

BRACKLEY
Early closing Wednesday; market day Friday.

Brackley is one of a number of comfortable market towns to be found in Northamptonshire. It has much history: here the barons gathered to present their demands to King John's envoys and medieval tournaments were held near the town at Baynard's Green (now Bear's Green). During the fourteenth century the town enjoyed great prosperity as a staple for wool but by Leland's day it had become shrunken and poverty stricken.

In 1484 William of Waynflete bought the Hospital of St James and St John and gave it to his Oxford foundation of Magdalen College and during the following century the college was often evacuated to Brackley at times of plague in the university city. The connection is perpetuated in the name of the former grammar, now comprehensive school.

The Spectacle, a folly near Boughton village.

Until the Reform Bill of 1832 the ancient borough returned two members to Parliament, the 33 electors being in the Duke of Bridgewater's pocket. It continued as a municipal borough with a mayor and corporation until 1974, when it was taken into the new South Northamptonshire District, but it still retains its mayor and town council.

A bypass has taken the through traffic out of the wide tree-lined High Street, which has for a centrepiece the free-standing Town Hall built by the Duke of Bridgewater in 1706. Coaching days are recalled by the Plough and Crown inns. The almshouses built in 1633 were in 1970 converted into flats.

The Old Town, lower and nearer the river Great Ouse, above which Brackley stands, has the parish church of St Peter nestling in a cul-de-sac. It is believed that the town started here and around the castle which once stood beside the Hinton Road. The main part of the town came later as trade and traffic increased along the Oxford to Northampton road.

Today there is a considerable industrial estate beside the A422 Buckingham road and new housing estates have boosted the population from little more than three thousand in 1961 to over seven thousand. This has happened without robbing the old town of its character.

BRAUNSTON

Braunston lies beside the Warwickshire border and apart from its canal history it has many interesting aspects. In the seventeenth century the following rhyme was current:
  'Braunston, Barby and Crick
  Worth a bishopric.'
It relates to the time when the fat lands of

48

Northamptonshire augmented the meagre emoluments of the Bishop of St Davids in Wales.

John Hassall in his *Tour of the Grand Junction Canal* in 1819 was struck by the prominence of the village, a thoroughfare place strung along a ridge about 400 feet (120 metres) above sea level, with a sharp descent to the canal. He wrote: 'the protruding objects above the village — the church, with a spire of 150 feet [46 metres] in length, a busy mill and some noble timber — broke the formality of the line and gave a picturesque character to one of the sweetest scenes in nature.' The mill has now been truncated into a dwelling and the church was rebuilt in 1849 but the general effect remains.

With its easy road links with Daventry and Rugby and the presence of light industries in the village Braunston continues to thrive.

BRIGSTOCK

Rockingham Forest was once divided into three bailiwicks: Brigstock, Rockingham and Cliffe. The first named, lying beside Harper's Brook, has always been a place of consequence in its neighbourhood (chapters 2, 4, 7). Once it had a market but by 1623 that was 'utterly decayed', although the market cross lingers and there is still a suggestion of a central precinct in the village. The Woodland Pytchley Hunt kennels are here.

At the edge of Harry's Park Wood, 1¼ miles (2 km) from Brigstock on a broad bridleway (OS 141; SP 950875), is a curious monument known as the Bocase Stone. It is only 3 feet (1 metre) high but has two inscriptions reading 'In this plaes grew Bocase Tree' and 'Here stood Bocase Tree'. There are several theories about the significance of the tree, in one of which Robin Hood figures. Another is that Bocase is a corruption of 'bow-cast', where local men assembled to practise archery, but as in the case of many traditions nothing is certain.

BRIXWORTH

This large village with a very famous church (chapter 4) has been chosen as a 'key centre' and has grown accordingly, with a population of around three thousand.

Much of its history was bound up with the Pytchley Hunt, whose headquarters were there from 1810 until 1967, when a new complex of kennels and stables was built about a mile away, adjacent to the old Market Harborough railway line. The names of Kennel Terrace and Hunt Cottage on the Spratton Road are a reminder of the hunt's former whereabouts and many famous people are recalled: 'Squire' Osbaldeston, who was once the Master; 'Honest Jack', Viscount Althorp, who would post down overnight from his

Market cross, Brigstock.

parliamentary duties to go out with the hunt in the morning; and professionals such as Frank Freeman, whose expertise was such that it was said of him that 'Hounds were a useless expense, Frank could catch a fox without one.' There used to be many ancillary establishments including a saddler, a bootmaker and a tailor who made 'pink' coats. All are gone, replaced by light industry, but most of the inhabitants of the spreading housing estates find occupation elsewhere, as is the case with the majority of Northamptonshire villages today.

BROUGHTON

The largest village in the extended borough of Kettering, Broughton is now bypassed by the A43 road. Most of its buildings are modern but the Yeoman's House in the main street is a seventeenth-century listed structure.

Broughton is best known because of the curious custom of ushering in the patronal festival on the first Sunday after 12th December by a midnight parade of a 'tin-can band'. In 1929 the parish council attempted to stop the cacophony with threats of prosecution and sixty participants were summoned to Kettering magistrates court, arriving there in two charabancs, while the town band played and marched with them to the court house. They were all fined and bound over but the whole business was so surrounded by ridicule that no further attempts were made to stop the custom and it has carried on to this day.

BUGBROOKE

The *Whellan's Directory* of 1874 listed two prominent citizens of Bugbrooke: the Reverend J. H. Harrison MA and Robert Heygate, farmer and miller of Bugbrooke Mill. The former was a 'squarson' — squire and parson. There were further generations of the Harrisons but they have now ended.

The Heygates, however, continue and their huge mill buildings dominate the local landscape. Villages such as Bugbrooke in the upper Nene valley have always been relatively large, being founded on a sound agricultural base, and Bugbrooke is a 'key village' so it has more than doubled its size since 1961 to about 2500.

From the village Baptist church sprang the Jesus Fellowship, a revivalist Christian movement which has had considerable impact on the neighbourhood in a variety of ways, including the creation of a chain of shops selling health foods.

BURTON LATIMER

A compact small town adjacent to the river Ise, Burton Latimer has grown to a population of about 5500 and has been taken into the enlarged Borough of Kettering. In addition to its noble church (chapter 4), it has two manor houses, one next to the church and Burton Latimer Hall on the outskirts towards Kettering. The suffix to the town's name comes from William de Latimer who held that manor in 1280. The Harpur family have owned Burton Latimer Hall since 1760 and their home is a handsome Jacobean structure with a large dovecote of the same period built in Weldon stone.

The town possesses much that is modern: a health centre, library, fire station and recreation centre. Two firms of international standing provide employment — Weetabix and Alumasc — in addition to the traditional footwear industry.

Some distance from the town on the A510 from Finedon to Thrapston but within the parish boundary is the Round House. It was built by General Arbuthnot, who entertained the Duke of Wellington at nearby Woodford House and who was told by the Duke that the local terrain reminded him of the battlefield of Waterloo.

CLIPSTON

This is a pleasantly sequestered village 4 miles (6 km) south of Market Harborough. In Victorian times it was described as 'large and respectable' but has now much shrunk in population. Its most notable feature is the Free Grammar School and Hospital, founded

by Sir George Buswell and built in 1668-73. The interior and back of the school were very much altered in 1926 but originally the centre of the building had the headmaster's lodging on the ground floor with the school room on the first floor and the hospital for twelve 'poor aged persons' in the two wings.

COLLINGTREE

Being 3 miles (5 km) south of Northampton, between the dual-carriageway A508 giving access to the M1 and the motorway itself, the village was taken into the borough when the latter enlarged in 1974. Before the building of the M1 Collingtree was a quiet village built mostly of stone and with a thatched inn called the Wooden Walls of Old England. Since then many pressures have ensued, including a huge 'leisure development' on a 275 acre (111 ha) site, embracing a health and leisure centre, a hotel, housing, a nursing home and a golf course.

CORBY

Early closing Wednesday; market days Friday and Saturday.

In 1930 Corby was a village of 1500 people but it has expanded into a town of fifty thousand by the growth of iron and steel making. Before nationalisation Stewarts and Lloyds used the local ironstone to produce steel tubes in the largest factory of its kind in Europe. A new civic centre was created and all seemed set fair when the closure of the steelworks in 1979 threatened to make Corby a ghost town. However, Corby's previous status as a steel town with a single industry qualified it for help from the European Economic Community so that thousands of jobs have been created by hundreds of companies relocated or started in the town and unemployment has fallen dramatically.

The town has much to offer its inhabitants. The leisure complex next to the Civic Centre, the Festival Hall and the theatre at the heart of the town are only some of the modern facilities to be enjoyed. Only 1½ miles (2.5 km) from the town centre is the nature reserve of King's Wood, 77 acres (31 ha) of ancient oak and ash woodland.

Amidst its brave new growth Corby clings to one ancient tradition — the 'Pole Fair', held every twenty years at Whitsuntide, 1982, 2002 and so on. An exception was made in 1985 to celebrate the four hundredth anniversary of the charter granted by Queen Elizabeth I.

DALLINGTON

Considering that Dallington is little more than a mile from the centre of Northampton and was taken into the borough in 1932, it is surprising that it has kept so much of its village character. It is a conservation area and the open fields and woods to the west and Dallington Park to the south have protected it from urbanisation. The thirteenth-century church, the brook beside the green, with the Old Forge, almshouses and village hall grouped against a background of mature trees, and the eighteenth-century Wheatsheaf Inn not far away all create a pleasing rural atmosphere.

DAVENTRY

Early closing Thursday; market day Tuesday.

Like Brackley, Daventry is an ancient market town on an important road (Daventry is on the A45 Holyhead road), but Daventry's expansion has been the more dramatic, from less than six thousand in 1961 to nearly seventeen thousand in 1987. It has been bypassed twice and has a revised road system and a large industrial estate at each end. Those who knew only the old 'Daintree', as it was called, would be astonished to see it now.

Yet much of the old town has survived. The market place, the church of the Holy Cross (chapter 4), the eighteenth-century Moot Hall and the Gothic memorial cross remain at the centre. The last named, built in 1908, commemorates E. C. Burton, solicitor, clerk to the county magistrates and a sporting hero who in 1860 won the first National Hunt steeplechase.

Sheaf Street, along which the traffic of the Holyhead road once rolled, has been pedestrianised and the shops in it have been refurbished while the historic Wheatsheaf Inn (chapter 9) has been restored without robbing it of its character, so that the period charm of the town has been retained.

DEANSHANGER

Separated from north Buckinghamshire only by the river Great Ouse, Deanshanger is seen from afar because of the plume of smoke rising from the chimney of the Oxide Works, a large and highly automated factory producing synthetic iron oxide. It is on the site of an earlier industrial enterprise, that of E. and H. Roberts, which manufactured agricultural implements for over a century up to its closure in 1927. The village was helped into its early industrialisation by the presence of the Buckingham arm of the Grand Junction Canal, cut at the behest of the Marquess of Buckingham in 1800. Some of the products of E. and H. Roberts, such as ploughs and elevators, are still to be seen in farm museums and similar places.

Like most villages in the locality, Deanshanger was a centre for the cottage industry of bone lace making. Through the later nineteenth century Jesse and James Compton, father and son, were well known for their skill in making bobbins and produced the useful and decorative bone and wooden objects that are now collectors' pieces. In common with other south Northamptonshire villages Deanshanger has more than doubled in population since the late 1950s and it has its own comprehensive school, Kingsbrook, called after a stream that flows down from Whittlebury Forest. The triangular green with a row of former almshouses is a neat feature bordering the main road.

DESBOROUGH

A small, clean industrial town with a

Barkers shoe factory at Earls Barton, opened in 1987.

population of over six thousand, Desborough is part of the pattern of shoe towns along the Ise and Nene valleys and is pleasantly situated on high ground overlooking the former river. The main railway line from St Pancras skirts it and its name is associated with one of the most famous and beautiful of iron age relics, the Desborough mirror, whose curvilinear patterns have appeared in many history books. The original is in the British Museum and a replica can be seen in Northampton Central Museum.

Desborough grew in the nineteenth century under the impact of the shoe trade and had over 4000 people by 1911. Now the manufacture of footwear has diminished but, like other 'quality' shoemakers, Cheaneys of Desborough still continues.

DUSTON

Standing on a terrace above the Nene valley, Duston has always been a preferred area of settlement. Neolithic remains and a Roman centre, with a road running to join the Watling Street near Daventry at the station called *Bannaventa,* show that life flourished here long before the rise of Northampton, which swallowed the village after much protest in 1965. Ironstone quarrying went on along both sides of the Weedon road (under which there were tunnels) between 1845 and 1909, with consequent lowering of the terrain. One part of this is now the Westgate Industrial Area and another has been very useful as a 'civic amenity site' — a rubbish tip. In late Victorian times no less than five different kinds of building stone were extracted locally. Nearer the present the British Timken factory for making roller bearings, set up hurriedly because of dire wartime needs in the 1940s, has played a spectacular part in the place, including funding the British Timken Show between 1945 and 1978. New roads and wide-spreading housing estates have now largely integrated Duston with greater Northampton.

EARLS BARTON

In the twelfth century the manor of Barton was held by David, Earl of Huntingdon, hence the prefix, but long before his day the famous church tower (chapter 4) had been built on its hilltop overlooking the Nene valley. Below, the new A45, the Nene Valley Way, has relieved the village of much traffic.

Tanning of hides was established by the thirteenth century and continued until 1984 but the traditional boot and shoe industry is still carried on, a new factory being opened in 1987 by Barkers of Earls Barton. It employs four hundred shoe makers, producing 300,000 pairs of hand-lasted and hand-sewn shoes annually.

With its convenient situation and general prosperity Earls Barton has grown in population from less than three thousand in 1961 to about 4700.

The village Historical Society has compiled a 'historical walkabout', published by the county Library and Leisure Committee. This describes and illustrates 21 buildings or items of interest, including the custom of eating leek pie on Shrove Tuesday, a practice which has led to local folk being known as 'Barton Leeks'.

FINEDON

The first syllable of the name derives from the Anglo-Scandinavian word *thing,* meaning 'assembly', suggesting that Finedon was a centre of some importance at an early date, but its relative status declined so that it ceased to be a separate urban district in 1935 and was taken into Wellingborough. Its population is just over four thousand.

Finedon has a number of historic structures, some with features resulting from the eccentric efforts of the Dolben and Mackworth-Dolben families, formerly of Finedon Hall. At the crossroads in the centre is a small pyramidal pillar which once had mileages on it, put there by Sir English Dolben to celebrate the 'many blessings of 1789'. These probably included the recovery of George III from an attack of insanity and the birth of Louisa, a Dolben daughter.

William Mackworth-Dolben (1806-72) decorated or changed a number of buildings, including a former windmill in Station Road, which he capped with an embattled parapet, and the Bell Inn, given a mock Gothic front in 1872. Although the family has gone, their name is perpetuated in Mackworth Green, a pleasant quadrangle of ironstone cottages. The hall also had the mock Gothic treatment but was falling into ruin when it was restored and converted into smaller dwellings. Finedon possesses the oldest Friends' meeting house in the county, built in 1691.

Occupations once commonly followed were ironstone 'getting' and the footwear trade. In the nineteenth century a more unusual one was that of drying apples, before other means of preservation were available. Tough-skinned fruit were reduced by baking and pressing to a form like a thick biscuit and these were traded far until the business died in the 1870s. Most of the inhabitants, including those living in the several small modern housing estates, now travel to work.

FOTHERINGHAY

For Fotheringhay Castle see chapter 3, and for the church of St Mary and All Saints see chapter 4.

GEDDINGTON

This is a large village with a population of over twelve hundred and an attractive centre where the Eleanor Cross (chapter 5) stands away from the main road.

On the skyline is Geddington Chase, part of the residue of the forest where medieval kings hunted from their lodge in the village. This stood behind the churchyard adjacent to Wood Road and must have been sumptuous in its heyday for thirteenth-century documents refer to 'paintings in the King's chamber', of a second chapel to be built and of mews to be made for the King's falcons.

The medieval bridge over the Ise, with large cut-waters on one side, has been much repaired and carried the main road until about 1920, when the 'new' road was built. There has been much new building and the recreation area and extended village hall cater for most sports while industrial sites have been provided in Grange Road.

GRAFTON REGIS

Grafton Regis is easily passed through on the main road with nothing seen to indicate its eventful history. In the early 1960s a medieval hermitage was excavated on the west side of the road and floor tiles in the chapel bore the Woodville crest (chapter 9). In the church are tombs of this unhappy family and of the Fitzroys, for here is the origin of the title of the Dukes of Grafton; bestowed by Charles II on his natural son. Long before this Henry VIII had made Grafton the head of an honour, a huge estate covering most of south Northamptonshire and a convenient centre for hunting. Here was a house described in the reign of Charles I as 'the best and bravest seat in the Kingdom, a seat for a prince and not for a subject'. In December 1643, when held for the King by Sir John Digby, it came under siege from much superior Parliamentary forces from Newport Pagnell and Northampton and after its surrender on Christmas Eve the Roundheads burned the house down 'for the prevention of future inconveniences'. Later the remains were made into a farmhouse and nineteenth-century improvements made it a suitable residence for Colonel George Fitzroy, who lived there for about fifty years. The house is now used as a rehabilitation unit for people with head injuries.

GRAFTON UNDERWOOD

Less than one hundred people live in this village but it is attractive enough to be designated a conservation area. As its name implies, it is close to Rockingham Forest and surprisingly in its high position has a little stream running beside its main street. The disused airfield north of the village was the home of the 384th Bombardment Group of the United States Air Force and the base from where the first and last bombing missions to Europe were made by the 8th Army AF. A memorial to the group has been placed a quarter of a mile (400 metres) from the village on the road to Geddington.

GREAT WELDON

With its adjoining hamlet of Little Weldon (separated only by a brook) this large village is almost joined to Corby on its western side. Its long industrial history may go back to Roman times for a villa excavated in Chapel Field in 1955-6 had a circular workshop containing a furnace possibly used for ironworking. Great Weldon is famous for its stone quarries, of which John Bridges wrote early in the eighteenth century: 'Here are very ancient stone quarries of so hard a texture as to admit a polish almost equal to Italian marble. Many slabs and chimney-pieces in some of the principal houses are made of this stone.' He also mentioned a tradition that Old St Paul's Cathedral before the Great Fire was built of it.

Being close to Rockingham Forest, this village was once called Weldon-in-the-Woods and a lantern tower in the church of St Mary was a guide to travellers through the forest. Other interesting buildings are the circular lock-up on the green, with a conical roof capped by a stone orb, and Haunt Hill House. The origin of the strange name is a mystery but it is known that the house was built about 1636 by Humphrey Frisby, a local master mason. It

The obelisk at Finedon.

has a chimney stack on the axis of the house and a design of massive symmetry. Pevsner sees a likeness to houses in the region of Halifax and Huddersfield.

HIGHAM FERRERS

Although an ancient borough with a mayor and corporation and returning an MP until 1832, Higham was little more than a village in size until, in common with its neighbours and other towns along the A6 road to Bedford, it grew with the impact of the shoe industry. Even then the Crown and the Fitzwilliam family, the principal landowners, would not sell sites for factories so these were built in other places such as Rushden nearby. In this way the past has been preserved to a remarkable degree.

Today it is a busy little town of just over five thousand people which has lost some of its traffic since it was bypassed by the A45. Its abundance of good architecture is detailed in a *Historical Tour* published by the county Libraries and Leisure Services. This leads past the thirteenth-century market cross; the remains of the Coneygarth (rabbit warren) appertaining to the castle once owned by the Ferrers family and sited north of the church; the Saffron Moat fishpond dug for the fellows of the college founded by Archbishop Chichele in 1422 — so called because of the cultivation of saffron nearby, probably for use in the dispen-

The Bede House, Higham Ferrers.

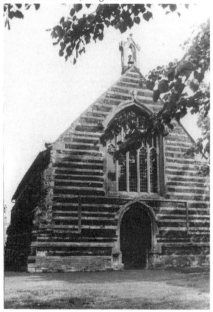

sary; and the famous complex of buildings mostly associated with Higham's greatest son, Henry Chichele.

Henry Chichele rose from obscurity to become Archbishop of Canterbury from 1414 to 1443 and founder of All Souls' College, Oxford, and to merit a magnificent tomb in Canterbury Cathedral. The remains of his college at Higham are on the left of the street named after it, going towards Kettering. The approach to the other buildings is from the Market Square past the churchyard cross to reach the Chantry Chapel, the Bede House with its conspicuous bands of contrasting stone (now used as a parish hall) and above all the mighty spire, one of the many to lift our eyes in this locality. (For the church see chapter 4.) They comprise as fine a group of ancient ecclesiastical buildings as can be found outside a cathedral city.

IRCHESTER

As its name suggests, this large village of about five thousand people has Roman connections. To the north-west of the Irchester turn on the A45 is Chester House and the township of Roman times lay to the east of this, alongside the trunk road. When the A45 was re-aligned in the early 1980s Roman relics came to light, including a large jar with a great hoard of coins, and these are to be found in the Central Museum at Northampton. Little Irchester, alongside the A509, grew up in the nineteenth century when ironstone quarrying began and part of the quarry is now the country park (chapters 2, 7).

The main village has grown quickly and has recreation fields, a village hall, a youth centre and other modern facilities, while the noble broach spire of St Katherine's church soars above all.

IRTHLINGBOROUGH

Once known in the vernacular as 'Artleborough', this town on the A6 has a population of over five thousand but has less to show for its long history than the nearby and similarly sized Higham Ferrers. It does have a remarkable church (chapter 4) and the remains of a market cross. The shaft of this has been used as a 'standard for adjusting the provincial pole', by which the 'doles' or portions in grazing meadows were measured.

Once blast-furnaces operated here because of the large ironstone deposits but industry now is of the lighter kind and includes the making of footwear. The town is well endowed with public facilities.

The A6 road crossing of the Nene on the way to Higham has been raised up so that one can look down on the medieval bridge of ten arches, which may date from the fourteenth century.

Wicksteed Park, Kettering.

KETTERING
Early closing Thursday; market day Saturday.
Until the rapid growth of Corby and Wellingborough Kettering was the second largest town in Northamptonshire (after Northampton) and its population has now reached nearly 45,000. It is halfway along the 'shoe belt' that stretches from Market Harborough in Leicestershire to beyond Rushden and the Bedfordshire border.

In Roman times there was a settlement on a site in north Kettering where the ironstone which has more recently played a part in the growth of the town was exploited. Henry III granted Kettering a charter as a market town in 1227. During the seventeenth century woollen products such as 'Shaloons, seyes and Tammies' were made and in the eighteenth the Eayre family cast bells in their foundry and gained repute as clockmakers. At the end of that century a factory was set up to prepare leather for the hand-sewn shoes made by workers at home but as at Northampton it was in the later nineteenth century that the burgeoning boot and shoe trade caused major expansion, the census figures for 1871 and 1911 being 7184 and 29,976 respectively.

The church (chapter 4) and Wicksteed Park (chapter 8) are notable features by any standards. The Alfred East Art Gallery is described in chapter 6. The town is pleasantly situated above the river Ise with much open country nearby.

Like Northampton, the town has always been strong for nonconformity. The Fuller Baptist church was founded in 1696, the Toller United Reform church dates from 1723 and in the Mission House in Lower Street in 1792 William Carey and others founded the Baptist Missionary Society, leading to his great work in India.

Among the many business enterprises in Kettering there is a remarkable firm of publishers, the Quince Tree Press, which operates from the back bedroom of the house of J. L. (Jim) Carr, the novelist, and is his creation. It has produced many attractive maps of various counties and 'little books' on a great variety of subjects.

KING'S CLIFFE
As its name suggests, this was a royal manor and since it gave its name to one of the three bailiwicks of Rockingham Forest it must have been a place of some importance in days gone by. It had a charter for a weekly market, which fell into disuse, and a three-day fair. In the nineteenth century it was still termed a 'pretty large village' but its population has now shrunk to less than a thousand.

In Victorian times there was a flourishing trade in wood carving and turning here, no less than ten of these craftsmen being listed in the directory of 1874. The tradition lived on in the name of the former inn, the Turners' Arms.

The village was also notable as the birthplace of William Law, a 'celebrated polemical and nonjuring divine' (1686-1761). He was

55

once famous as the author of such works as *The Serious Call* and left the Library House and Almshouses in Bridge Street to his native place. Much of this pleasant spot is a conservation area.

KING'S SUTTON

The delightful village of King's Sutton has always been important in its locality. King William I held the manor in 1086 and it was once the head of a hundred that included Brackley. It stands above the Cherwell, only the river separating it from Oxfordshire, and has many attractive features.

The precinct called the Square facing the church (chapter 4) is a fine centrepiece to the extensive village, with the Jacobean manor house, an older half-timbered court house and other handsome buildings surrounding the well kept green, all contributing to an effect enhanced by the stocks near the Bell Inn.

Despite being one of only two villages in the county now possessing a railway station, King's Sutton has not been hit by new development, but the building of the M40 motorway close at hand may cause a change.

LONG BUCKBY

This is one of the two villages in the county with a railway station, being on the Northampton to Rugby route. As the name suggests, it is a thoroughfare village and it has a population of over three thousand. There are some good old properties around the market place and nearby two very commodious places of worship, the Congregational Chapel dated 1771 and the Baptist one of 1846, both in the classical style and seating 700 and 600 respectively.

Buckby Wharf, 2 miles (3 km) south-west on the Grand Union Canal, was locally an important *entrepôt* and is still well used by pleasure craft.

MIDDLETON CHENEY

The largest village in the South Northamptonshire District lies astride the A422 Brackley-Banbury road and stretches as far north as the Banbury Lane. As it is only 2 miles (3 km) from the county boundary it looks to the Oxfordshire town rather than to Northampton. Like its outlying hamlet of Overthorpe, a mile (1.5 km) to the west, the centre of the place is a conservation area. Among the old houses are some with traditional craft associations, tanning, weaving of hosiery and clockmaking. New housing estates have boosted the population to over three thousand, so that numerous facilities include the Chenderit comprehensive school. Pupils from here helped the warden compile the guide to the Farthinghoe Nature Trail (chapter 2).

NORTHAMPTON

Early closing Thursday; market days Wednesday and Saturday.

As in most cases, Fuller had appropriate words when describing the county town. Explaining why scholars from Oxford and Cambridge set up a short-lived university about 1260, he called it 'so convenient a place, where the air is clear, and not over-sharp; the earth fruitful, yet not over-dirty; water is plentiful, yet free from any fennish annoyance'.

When the scholars came it was one of the six most prosperous towns in England and its 245 acres (99 ha) made it third in size only to London and Norwich. Unhappily by 1484 it was a scene of 'desolation and ruin'.

Other than the churches, visual evidence of this long and chequered past is not conspicuous. Like the castle, many old buildings have disappeared. Some of this is attributable to the great fire of 1675 but there are other reasons. In about 1960 Pevsner likened the Market Square to the great market places of the Low Countries and noticed the Victorian cast iron fountain at its centre, the seventeenth-century Peacock Hotel, the Emporium Arcade of 1901 and the Welsh House adjoining in Newland, one of the few that escaped the great fire. Of these the Welsh House is the only survivor and that only as a facade to a new building. The north side of the square is now dominated by large new buildings, of which the Grosvenor Shopping Centre is most prominent. For those who like to buy goods under modern conditions this has much to recommend it. Peacock Way, the shopping precinct that took the place of the historic inn, has been demolished after only twenty years.

An *Historic Town Trail* has been published by the Borough Council, starting from All Saints — a splendid centrepiece to the town from which all the principal streets radiate — and going by the Lutyens war memorial; the Sessions House (one of the first buildings built after the fire); the Royal Theatre in Guildhall Road designed by C. J. Phipps in 1884 with an archetypal Victorian auditorium inside; 78 Derngate, a house remodelled in 1916 by Charles Rennie Mackintosh for the modelmaker W. J. Bassett-Lowke; Becket's Well, where traditionally the Archbishop rested after his flight from the castle (see chapter 3) in 1164; the original buildings of the General Hospital, which were in fields when new; St Giles's School, a Victorian Gothick structure now refurbished and adapted for use as a church community centre; the partly pedestrianised Abington Street, where a new metal sculpture shows children playing on a giant shoe-repairer's last (this has caused pain to purists because it represents the work of a 'cobbler' rather than that of the expert shoemaker known as a 'snob'); the Victorian

(Left) *Statue in Abington Street, Northampton.*
(Right) *Express Lifts tower, Northampton.*

Guildhall, which has been likened to a Venetian *palazzo*; and the various churches and museums (chapters 4 and 6).

In Marefair at the oldest end of the town, known as 'the Boroughs' and mostly utterly changed by development, is Hazelrigg House, built in 1662 for the family of that name and another rare survivor from the fire. Although handsome, it is somewhat dilapidated but plans exist to make it into offices.

All this, except the hospital, is within the limits of the medieval town, three-quarters of which, amounting to six hundred houses, was destroyed by the fire, but such efforts were made that within ten years the town was 're-edified and nobly improved' and homes provided for four thousand people. No trace remains of the fabric of the town walls but their outline can be discerned from the street plan.

In the eighteenth century the town was an important coaching centre. One of the main routes was to Hockliffe via Newport Pagnell and Woburn. Many coaches called at inns such as the George, the Peacock and the Angel so that they prospered and during this period a number of innkeepers became mayors of the town.

By the time of the first census in 1801 the population had risen to seven thousand and during the nineteenth century Northampton expanded from its former confines so that by 1900 the village of Kingsthorpe, about 2 miles (3 km) from the town centre, had been taken into the borough. In the 1930s, when the town was the world's biggest centre for the making of men's footwear, another 2700 acres (1092 ha) were absorbed. About 1953 the large King's Heath estate, planned with what was then the latest expertise, was laid out north of Dallington.

In 1965 the villages of Duston and Weston Favell were included within the Borough, along with the suburbs of Whitehills and Boothville.

With the coming of the Development Corporation Great and Little Billing to the east, Great Houghton, Hardingstone, Wootton and Collingtree to the south were all absorbed and the massive Eastern and Southern Developments were set in motion, and by 1986 the number of people in Northampton was thought to be above 170,000.

A strong tradition of nonconformity (in every sense) has prevailed in Northampton since the time of the Lollards, who were very active here. From 1571 onwards All Saints was the scene of Puritan 'prophesyings'. In 1729

Delapre Abbey, Northampton.

Doctor Philip Doddridge, the Independent preacher and hymn writer, established his theological academy in Sheep Street. A later independent was the atheist Charles Bradlaugh, MP for the town for eleven years and one of the most controversial figures ever to enter the House of Commons.

The Borough Library in Abington Street possesses many relics of John Clare (chapter 9) and every issue of one of the oldest continuously published newspapers to be found. The *Northampton Mercury* began in 1720 and still appears under the title of *Mercury and Herald.*

The town is well blessed with municipal parks. The Racecourse (formerly Northampton Heath), Abington Park, Delapre, Becket's Park (still sometimes called Cow Meadow) and others smaller ring the town. The Eastern Development has Lings Wood and the Southern Hunsbury. Near the latter is Danes Camp Leisure Centre.

Equally numerous are the supermarkets on the fringe and the great 'employment areas' on the outer perimeter of the town: Brack Mills on the Bedford Road, Moulton Park on the site of a medieval hunting park and others provide jobs. Much older than these but with a structure that is more conspicuous than any is the Express Lifts factory off the Weedon Road, with its 418 foot (127 metre) high tower, facetiously known as the 'Northampton lighthouse'.

Along with all this there has been an educational expansion at the Nene College and the College of Further Education so that the old town seems set to keep thriving and growing into the twenty-first century.

For the battlefield of Northampton see chapter 8, and for Delapre Abbey see chapter 5.

OUNDLE
Early closing Wednesday; market day Thursday.

To get a good distant impression of Oundle approach it along the old A605 road from Thrapston. From there is seen the grouping of grey stone buildings with the delicate 208 foot (63 metre) spire outreaching all, still looking somewhat as Leland saw it, 'buildid of stone as almost al the Tounes be of Northamptonshire'. The church is described in chapter 4.

Crossing the Nene and passing a marina where pleasure cruisers are built one gets a whiff of the Fens, which are at no great distance. Oundle was and is a 'clean, regular and compact market town', with a population of over three thousand, little bigger than it was a century ago.

In 1554 Sir William Laxton, grocer, was Lord Mayor of London and in 1556 he founded a grammar school and almshouse in his native town. This became in the late nineteenth and early twentieth century the well known Oundle School, largely owing to the efforts of F. W. Sanderson, a strong headmaster.

The market bell is rung at midday on Thursday to signify the continuance of Oundle's function as an ancient market town. A former Congregational church is now the Stahl Theatre. Victoria Hall can seat three hundred and in it is held the annual Gilbert and Sullivan opera and other functions.

The eastern bypass has eased the flow of

traffic and much of Oundle is a conservation area. Also it has been chosen by the Department of the Environment for its Historic Towns Scheme so it should be safe from harm.

A town guide with two town trails is available from the information office (chapter 12). Among much else this tells the curious story of the 'Drummingwell', which gave its name to the lane behind the Talbot Inn. Before the later eighteenth century the well at times made a loud noise like a marching rhythm, which was thought then to presage calamities such as the Great Fire of London. But having ceased to 'drum', it was filled in so that only the name remains.

PAULERSPURY

West of the Watling Street, Paulerspury has a mile-long High Street leading to the church of St James, which is beside a pleasant green. In it are fourteenth-century oaken effigies, supposedly Sir Laurence de Pavely and his wife. This family gave the village the first part of its name, the -pury suffix meaning a pear tree, as does that of the next village along the A5, Potterspury, where kilns of medieval and later times have been excavated.

Also in the church is the extraordinary early seventeenth-century monument to Sir Arthur Throckmorton and his wife, who are gazing lovingly at each other. He was the brother of Raleigh's Bess and left a detailed account of the manor house he built with infinite care. None of the fabric remains above ground.

Paulerspury was one of the forest villages of Whittlewood and exemplifies their type by its fragmented nature, covering a wide area with its outliers, such as Pury End, Tews End and Plumpton End. In earlier times it bred a hardy race of poachers. A local tradition says that they hid the carcases of the deer inside two tombs with heavy tops in the churchyard or under the bridges on the Watling Street, from where they were smuggled up to London by a carrier who sold them there. Conflict raged between the poachers and the keepers, sometimes with dire results to one side or the other. One keeper was ambushed on his way to Towcester market and found lying dead in Tews End Lane, while his pony went home alone.

Paulerspury is also notable as the birthplace of William Carey (chapter 9) and the head-quarters of the Grafton Hunt. Among the interesting buildings are the premises of the Sir Henry Royce museum (chapter 6) and a Victorian primary school which has been said to be 'wildly Gothic' on account of its elaborate construction.

RAUNDS

This small but growing industrial town (population over six thousand) has been termed 'the home of the British army boot'. The shoemakers have always been an independent race and at the time of the Enclosure Award (1794-6) there were riots here. Again, in 1905, long before the Jarrow march, the bootmakers of Raunds were represented by 115 of their number who set off for London to try to get a better deal from the War Office. Their march was organised with military preci-

Market Square, Oundle.

sion by Northampton-born James Gribble, a former regular soldier and activist in the early days of the Labour movement, and they were acclaimed on their way.

Raunds lies in a secondary valley of the Nene close to the Cambridgeshire border and was once noted for a local stone called 'Rance rag', much in demand for mantelpieces. In the 1980s the town has become an important centre of archaeological research. The Raunds Project includes Saxon and medieval remains in the town itself, the Roman settlement at Stanwick, bronze age barrows near Irthlingborough and neolithic remains and a deserted village site at West Cotton. It is believed that all this will shed much new light on the history of this part of the Nene valley. See chapter 4 for the church.

ROTHWELL
Early closing Thursday; market day Monday.
Yet another A6 town, 'Rowell', as it is sometimes called, is an ancient market town with a population now grown to well over six thousand. It stands on a hillside above the Slade Brook and has a number of historic buildings. Among them are the Market House, built by Thomas Tresham and with some of his fantastic decoration; the church (chapter 4); the almshouses of the Jesus Hospital (founded 1591), which have been adapted to make viable modern dwellings, and the Georgian manor house that serves as council offices. The whole centre of the town is a conservation area.

The annual week-long charter fair originally granted by King John survives and a later version of the charter by James I is read out at various points in the town at 6 am on Trinity Monday by the lord of the manor's bailiff on horseback. This right is jealously guarded.

The town is very important in the history of nonconformity in the county, for the first Congregational meeting house began in a barn in 1655 and soon after people travelled from a wide area of other neighbouring counties to attend. The present Congregational (United Reform) church dates from 1735.

RUSHDEN
Like Northampton, but at a later date (1771), Rushden was decimated by fire so that the only notable buildings are the church (chapter 4) and Rushden Hall. Part of the latter goes back to the time of John of Gaunt, while the impressive east front is Jacobean. It comes into the story *Love for Lydia* by H. E. Bates, who was born and raised in the town, which is called 'Evensford' in the novel. His autobiographical *The Vanished World* is a vivid evocation of life there and in neighbouring places in the early years of the twentieth century. The hall stands in an attractive public park with a stream flowing through it and part of it is used by the East Northamptonshire District Council.

In addition to footwear manufacture Rushden has other light industries so that the town of nearly 23,000 inhabitants appears busy, prosperous and well-off for amenities. The Railway Station Museum is described in chapter 6.

SUDBOROUGH
Sudborough has had a long association with Rockingham Forest. In the year 1251 Henry, son of the shepherd John, was 'sitting eating his dinner under a hedge in the field of Sudborough' when William of Drayton came past in a green tunic with a bow and arrows and two other men likewise armed. There was also a man riding a black horse with a fawn on his lap, carrying venison behind him covered by leaves. At the rear came two lads leading eight greyhounds, 'of which some were white, some tawny and some red'. These colourful details are known from the proceedings of the Forest Courts, which among other commitments tried to keep down poaching.

A village with such long and close ties with Rockingham Forest is an appropriate home for an author whose writings about the county and elsewhere have been compared to those of Hudson and Jefferies. 'BB', or Denys Watkins-Pitchford, writer, artist, sportsman and naturalist, has cast a perceptive eye on the countryside of Northamptonshire and the creatures which inhabit it.

THRAPSTON
Early closing Thursday; market day Tuesday.
Though a small town of less than three thousand, Thrapston was granted a weekly market by King John in 1205 and in Victorian times had two railway stations, a cattle market, a corn exchange, a county court and a union workhouse.

A most noticeable feature today is the huge spread of water left by gravel extraction where there is a lakeside walk along the former Northampton to Peterborough railway line. To the west, where the A604 from Kettering to Huntingdon crosses the Nene, is the Nine Arches Bridge. This is only partly medieval because in 1795 five arches were destroyed by a great 'sea flood', as it was termed.

TOWCESTER
The name tells of its origin, for this was the site of *Lactodorum*, a Roman station on the Watling Street. Later it appears in the Anglo-Saxon Chronicle when Edward the Elder fortified it against the Danes, the Roman road being the frontier between Wessex and the Danelaw.

Between here and Old Stratford is one of the best stretches of what has been called the 'finest and most extensive Praetorian highway in the kingdom'. Despite the attentions of many road engineers, including Telford, the A5 still follows the straight Roman track for long distances. In coaching days many fast vehicles such as the 'Tally-ho' coaches raced along here and the Talbot and Saracen's Head inns were well known to travellers. The latter, for a time known as the Pomfret Arms, has been claimed as the 'well known sporting house' where Tom Brown enjoyed his breakfast on his first trip to Rugby and is almost certainly the inn described by Dickens in *Pickwick Papers*, where his best known character found refuge after a wet ride from Birmingham and where Pott and Slurk and their supporters had their fracas in the kitchen.

The opening of the M1 caused the constant flow of traffic along the A5 to dwindle for a time but in the long term Towcester has not suffered. The population has shown a steady increase to over five thousand.

Modern light industries such as microelectronics have moved in and a new industrial estate is planned in the Brackley Road. The A5 has become busy again as commuters hasten along it on their way to Milton Keynes and fast trains to London.

The town has some interesting buildings other than the church and the inns. At the centre is the Italianate Town Hall and Corn Exchange of 1865 — now the parish council headquarters — and in the Brackley Road the ironstone building formerly the workhouse. This was an early design by Sir George Gilbert Scott, whose father was the parson at Wappenham, a village nearby, where in 1833 he planned his first building — the Vicarage. His later achievements included the Martyrs' Memorial at Oxford, the Albert Memorial and St Pancras station and hotel.

Archdeacon Sponne (chapter 4) has given his name to the former grammar and now comprehensive school he originally founded. Also he caused to be built after his death the fifteenth-century Chantry House facing the little square by the town hall. This has been refurbished to make a parish office, meeting hall and kitchen.

The great house of the Fermor-Hesketh family, Easton Neston, designed by Hawksmoor, is immediately east of the town. The Fermors came here in 1528 and although the Earldom of Pomfret was lost by the disappearance of the direct line in 1867 the present Lord Hesketh can find much justification for his family motto *Hora et sempre* ('now and always'). Within his grounds is Towcester National Hunt racecourse and an imposing gate screen of 1822 marks the entrance to the course from the Watling Street.

The church at Weedon Bec.

WEEDON BEC

There are three parts to Weedon: Road Weedon on the Watling Street, Upper Weedon and Lower Weedon to the south. The church of St Peter with its Norman tower at Lower Weedon is cut off from the village in one direction by the railway viaduct on the main line from Euston and in the other by the embankment of the Grand Union Canal. The total population of the three parts is over two thousand. The name derives from the abbey of Bec Hellouin in Normandy, which held the manor in the twelfth century.

When England was under the threat of Napoleonic invasion Weedon with its central location and proximity to the new canal was used for a Royal Military Depot — a stronghold to which George III could retire — and extensive barracks were built with access to a canal wharf guarded by a portcullis. This military presence lingered until 1965 as an Ordnance Depot and some interesting buildings remain but their future seems uncertain.

WEEDON LOIS

Set in a mesh of lanes between the A5 and the A43 but well removed from both, Lois Weedon (as the residents prefer) is a very quiet place today but was once a magnet to many.

The name Weedon signifies 'a hill with a

temple' and presumably refers to a pagan sacred place. The Picardy family of Picquigny had their castle there, of which only the name Castle Hill survives. They founded and endowed a priory attached to the Benedictine abbey of St Lucien at Beauvais. The Hundred Years War led to the dispossession of foreign religious orders and in 1437 Henry Chichele, Archbishop of Canterbury, founded All Souls' College, Oxford, and this was partly endowed from Weedon Priory. The college still owns property here.

'Lois' or 'Loys' comes from St Lucien, some of whose relics found their way to the priory, so that it became a place of pilgrimage: Chaucer's Prioress mildly invoked St Loy. The monks discovered a mineral spring to the south of the church and as late as the eighteenth century people resorted to it: 'even blind and leprous people it infallibly cured', Morton declared. A pilgrims' hospice was pulled down in the reign of Elizabeth I and of all the fabric of this and the priory only a small summerhouse in the old vicarage grounds may have been part. The well is covered with a stone slab.

The nearby hamlet of **Weston by Weedon** has the Crown, an inn dating from the seventeenth century, Armada House, with its date of 1588, and a Baptist chapel (1791), for it was once a refuge for persecuted nonconformists. There is also Weston Hall, the home of the writer Sir Sacheverell Sitwell. His sister Edith Sitwell, the poet, is buried in Lois Weedon churchyard under a tombstone carved by Henry Moore depicting a pair of delicately beautiful hands and overlooking the remains of the monastic fishponds.

WELLINGBOROUGH

Market days Wednesday, Friday, Saturday.

There are many similarities between Wellingborough and Northampton. Throughout their histories both have been the focal point of a rural area. When Leland visited Wellingborough he found it 'a good quik Market Toune' and King John granted the first charter in 1201. Wellingborough had its great fire in 1738 when six hundred where made homeless, many of whom sheltered in All Hallows' church, which survived although the heat was so great that it melted the lead on the roof.

The coming of the Midland Railway in 1860 helped bring about an increase in population from 6382 in 1861 to 18,400 forty years later, in the same way that Northampton grew in those years.

At that time the boot and shoe industry was going over to mass production: the first factory opened in Sheep Street in 1851 and can still be seen opposite the Golden Lion Inn, although now converted into shops. For a time men refused to work machines for closing the uppers of footwear, so women entered the industry. Since 1961 Wellingborough has grown in a similar way to the county town by an influx of newcomers and the taking in of adjoining parishes so that the population has more than doubled from barely 30,000 to about 65,000. Likewise there have been created the Denington, Finedon Road and Park Farm industrial estates.

It should not be thought that Wellingborough is merely a smaller version of Northampton. In AD 948 King Aedred of Mercia gave much of the local land to the abbey of Croyland (now Crowland) and about 1320 the abbot began a swan farm in the area now known as Swanspool, where today there are delightful public gardens.

The town was early famed for its springs and wells and several appear on the arms of the borough, the most celebrated being the Red Well (so called because of the iron content), still to be seen in a meadow with the nearby White Well, a short way south of the eastern end of Kilborn Road. When royal visits occurred in 1628 and 1637 it seemed that the town might become a spa but this did not happen. About 1870 a local firm of brewers used the Red Well so that their 'celebrated ales and stout' might possess the 'stimulating medicinal qualities' of the water but it is not clear how the health of the town's drinkers was affected.

Wellingborough was Royalist in the Civil War and suffered for it. After a skirmish in which a Parliamentary officer was killed Roundheads from Northampton stormed the place and severe reprisals followed. Forty prisoners were taken, tied together in pairs and driven along the road to Northampton with the vicar, Master Jones, who was 'lame and sickly', mounted on a 'poor jade' behind. He was lodged in the castle prison, where he died.

The town appears more successful than Northampton in preserving its ancient buildings and other historic relics. It has kept two picturesque old inns, the Hind and the Golden Lion, at the town's heart. The fifteenth-century thatched ironstone tithe barn has been fully restored and used for various functions. Whereas the Victorian cast iron fountain on Northampton's Market Square has disappeared, the 'Jotto Page' fountain removed from Wellingborough town centre in 1955 has been re-sited at Swanspool. (James 'Jotto' Page gave the fountain to the town in 1903 to commemorate the coronation of Edward VII.)

One of the most agreeable features at Wellingborough is the Walks. These are tree-lined promenades, one of which was laid out as long ago as 1847 and the other more recently, along the banks of the Nene, where the river Ise joins its parent river. The town also

Tithe barn, Wellingborough.

possesses a public school which meta-
morphosed from an ancient grammar school
late in the nineteenth century.

In 1987 the Wellingborough Civic Society
opened the Heritage Centre (chapter 6).

In addition to being on the inter-city route
from St Pancras, Wellingborough is joined to
the M1 by the dual carriageway of the Nene
Valley Way, so should continue to flourish.

For shoppers Wellingborough enjoys the
great advantage of unlimited free parking and
the Arndale shopping centre is reckoned the
equal of most. The churches are described in
chapter 4.

WILBARSTON
Wilbarston has two of the oldest houses in
the county. In Barlow's Lane is a fifteenth-
century building with its ridge-pole still supported by the original cruck timbers. In
Church Lane there is a house of similar date
reputedly haunted by two ghosts — 'Sir
George' and a nun — until a former Bishop of
Peterborough entered the house, since when
they have been seen no more.

WOLLASTON
Along with a population of about three
thousand Wollaston has many of the attributes
of a small town. In 1985 a bypass relieved it of
the traffic flow along the A509. In addition to
the traditional footwear manufacture in build-

ings typical of the trade, which is still the
largest employer, there is a small modern
industrial estate and the Scott Bader firm in
and around Wollaston Hall. This organisation
supports the village with both employment and
recreational facilities.

The Wollaston Society is dedicated to the
preservation of the place and its historical
remains, such as Beacon Hill (chapter 3), from
where it is possible to see on a clear day 27
church spires (so it is said). Close to it is the
Wollaston Museum (chapter 6) housing local
bygones and the society annually revives an
old street market, usually in July. Wollaston
occupies a hilltop above the wide water-
meadows of the Nene and in common with
other riparian places a former cottage industry
was the making of rush mats, the raw material
being culled from the river.

WOODFORD HALSE
A large village of nearly two thousand
people, Woodford lives with the ghost of a
great railway enterprise. In the 1890s Britain's
last new main line — the Great Central — was
driven through the county, linking Nottingham
and London by an alternative route and
dividing the little village of Woodford Halse
and its hamlet of Hinton by the finest railway
construction yet seen. In addition Woodford
was chosen as the site for a depot and railway
junction, whereby it earned the nickname of

'Little Swindon'. Railwaymen were brought here from the Midlands, the population doubled and the engine sheds and marshalling yards, once described as the 'pride of Europe' gave rise to the notion that Woodford Halse would grow into a large town. But the line was closed in 1966 and now there remains only the 35 acre (14 ha) spread created by soil taken from the Catesby tunnel, two bridges, the terraced brick houses under the embankment

and memories of the time when 650 were employed by the railway and crack expresses such as the 'Master Cutler' thundered through on their way from Marylebone to Sheffield. The Great Central is no more than a great scar on the landscape and Woodford folk mostly seek employment in Daventry, Banbury or Northampton. They have the consolation that they are surrounded by a very peaceful and pleasant countryside.

11
Itineraries for motorists

Route 1. Northampton — Althorp — Great Brington — Brockhall — Flore — Newnham — Farthingstone — Fawsley — Badby — Daventry — Braunston — Ashby St Ledgers — West Haddon — Guilsborough — Holdenby — Northampton

Route 2. Northampton — Greens Norton — Syresham — Brackley — Croughton — Aynho — King's Sutton — Middleton Cheney — Sulgrave — Culworth — Byfield — Eydon — Canons Ashby — Bugbrooke — Northampton

Route 3. Northampton — Wootton — Courteenhall — Blisworth — Stoke Bruerne — Alderton — Paulerspury — Towcester — Silverstone — Whittlebury — Wicken — Deanshanger — Passenham — Cosgrove — Grafton Regis — Hartwell — Horton — Castle Ashby — Cogenhoe — Northampton

Route 4. Northampton — Abington — Weston Favell — Holcot — Brixworth — Cold Ashby — Naseby — Clipston — Kelmarsh — Lamport — Old-Walgrave — Moulton — Northampton.

Route 5. Higham Ferrers — Denford — Thrapston — Thorpe Waterville — Aldwincle — Grafton Underwood — Geddington — Newton-in-the-Willows — Rushton — Desborough — Rothwell — Earls Barton — Irchester — Higham Ferrers

Route 6. Oundle — Brigstock — Stanion — Great Oakley — Cottingham — Rockingham — Gretton — Kirby Hall — Deene — Bulwick — King's Cliffe — Wansford — Fotheringhay — Oundle

The village pump at East Haddon.

NORTHAMPTONSHIRE

* Country park, nature reserve etc. (Ch.2)
⊓ Site of archaeological interest (Ch.3)
+ Church (Ch.4)
▲ Historic building or garden (Ch.5)
M Museum (Ch.6)
I Industrial heritage (Ch.7)
O Other place to visit (Ch.8)
■ Town or village (Ch.10)

▲ Easton-on-the-Hill

R. Welland
* Wakerley Great Wood
■ King's Cliffe

I Harringworth   Fotheringhay + ⊓

Rockingham Castle
Kirby Hall
▲ Deene Park
Southwick Hall
M ■ Ashton

▲ Great Weldon
OUNDLE ■ +

CORBY ■
* M East Carlton
Lyveden New Bield ▲
I
+ ■
* I Brigstock
▲ Barnwell

Wilbarston ■
⊓ Newton
Triangular Lodge ▲ ■ Geddington
R. Nene
O Lilford Park

DESBOROUGH ■
Boughton House ■ Sudborough
* Titchmarsh Nature Reserve

■ Clipston
R. Ise
+ ■ ROTHWELL
Orton + Weekley + +
Warkton
■ Grafton
+ Lowick
Underwood
THRAPSTON

⊓ Sibbertoft
KETTERING ■
+ Barton Seagrave
* Denford
* Kinewell Lake

R. Avon
O Grange Lodge Mini Farm Park
M ▲ Kelmarsh Hall
O Naseby
OMI
■ Broughton
BURTON LATIMER
I Finedon
+ ■ RAUNDS

M1
Lamport Hall ▲
Faxton ⊓
IRTHLINGBOROUGH ■ + ■ HIGHAM FERRERS

⊓ Lilbourne
O Guilsborough Grange
OM
RUSHDEN ■

Coton Manor
Crick O
+ ■ Brixworth
WELLINGBOROUGH ■ +
Irchester
M45 Kilsby I
I Ravensthorpe Reservoir
I Reservoir
Holdenby House
* Pitsford Reservoir
MI * I
■ Sywell
* O

. Ashby St Ledgers ■ +
) Long Buckby ■
■ Boughton
M
+ ■ Earls Barton
M ■ Wollaston

I
Muscott ⊓
+ Great Brington
Althorp ▲
Billing ⊓ O *
I
Dallington ⊓ + I
■ Whiston

■ Braunston
NORTHAMPTON ■
+ Easton Maudit

DAVENTRY ■
* + ■ ⊓
Nether Heyford
Duston OM ▲
⊓
▲ + Castle Ashby

Staverton I
+ Dodford
I
Cliffords Hill
+ Denton •

Weedon Bec
■ Bugbrooke
O

Arbury Hill ⊓ * Badby Wood
+ Stowe-Nine-Churches
Collingtree

Charwelton I
* + Fawsley
⊓ Farthingstone
Blisworth
* < Salcey Forest

Woodford Halse ■
Canons Ashby
▲ +
■ Blakesley
R. Tove
I M Stoke Bruerne
M1

Weedon Lois ■
TOWCESTER ■ +
Grafton Regis ■

Paulerspury ■ Alderton
R. Great Ouse

O ▲ Edgcote House
I O Cosgrove
M

▲ Sulgrave Manor
* Bucknell Wood
▲

Stuchbury ⊓
I Helmdon
Wakefield Lodge
■ Deanshanger
+ ■ Passenham

+ ■ Middleton Cheney
■ BRACKLEY

* Farthinghoe

R. Cherwell
+ ■ King's Sutton
⊓ Rainsborough Camp
+ Croughton

▲
+ ■ Aynho

65

12
Tourist information centres

Corby: Civic Centre, George Street, Corby. Telephone: Corby (0536) 202551.

Kettering: The Coach House, Sheep Street, Kettering NN16 0AN. Telephone: Kettering (0536) 82143.

Northampton: 21 St Giles Street, Northampton NN1 1JA. Telephone: Northampton (0604) 22677.

Oundle: Market Hall, Market Place, Oundle PE8 4BA. Telephone: Oundle (0832) 74333

Northamptonshire County Leisure and Libraries Department: 27 Guildhall Road, Northampton NN1 1EF. Telephone: Northampton (0604) 20262.

The Northampton Borough Derngate Centre.

Index

Page numbers in italic refer to illustrations.

67